THE Heinemann *English* PROGRAMME 4

FOUNDATION

John Seely   David Kitchen

*with contributions from Clare Constant
and Frank Green*

Heinemann Educational Publishers
Halley Court, Jordan Hill, Oxford OX2 8EJ
A Division of Reed Educational & Professional Publishing Ltd

**OXFORD MELBOURNE AUCKLAND
JOHANNESBURG BLANTYRE GABORONE
IBADAN PORTSMOUTH (NH) USA CHICAGO**

© John Seely and David Kitchen 1996

The rights of John Seely and David Kitchen to be identified as
authors of this work have been asserted by them in accordance
with the Copyright, Designs and Patent Act.

First published 1996

2000 99 98
10 9 8 7 6 5 4 3

British Library Cataloguing in Publication data
for this title available from the British Library.

ISBN 0 435 10346 6

Designed and produced by Gecko Limited, Bicester, Oxon

Illustrations by Gerry Ball, Paul Davies, Paul Hampson,
Pantelas Palios, Brian Smith, Jamie Sneddon, Sam Thompson,
Katherine Walker, Dave Wood

Printed in Spain by Mateu Cromo

Acknowledgements

We should like to thank the following for permission to reproduce copyright material:

Gardeners' World Magazine for the extract from *Gardeners' World*, 6; Penguin Books
for the extract from *Mous 1* by Art Spiegelman, 6; The Independent Newspaper for TV
listings from *The Independent*, 6; Extract from *Timelines – Medicine*, first published in
the UK by Franklin Watts, a division of The Watts Publishing Group, London, © The
Salariya Book Company, 9, 10; Orion Publishing Group for the extract from *The Labours
of Herakles* by Kevin Crossley-Holland, 12; A P Watt Ltd for the extract from *Children of
the Gods* by Kenneth McLeish, 13; *The Spectator* for the extract by Tabitha Troughton,
14; the extract reprinted on p18 is from *Not So Stupid!* by Malorie Blackman, first
published by The Women's Press Ltd, 1990, 34 Great Sutton Street, London EC1V 0DX;
copyright © Joan Aiken Enterprises Ltd for the extract from *The Whispering Mountain*,
19; *The Daily Mail* and All Sport for the extract and photo, 21; *The Independent* and All
Sport for the extract and photo, 21; Mirror Syndication Group for two headlines and
extract from *The Daily Mirror*, 21, 22; The Birmingham Post for the newspaper extract,
22; The Star Newspaper for the extract, 22; The Sun Newspaper for the extract, 23; Hello
Magazine for extract A by James Bentley, 26; HarperCollins *Publishers* Limited for the
extract from *The Stories of Ray Bradbury* by Ray Bradbury (published by Grananda,
1983), 26; Aladdin Books Ltd for the extract from *Toxic Waste and Recycling* by Nigel
Hawkes (published by Franklin Watts, 1988), 29; MacDonald Young Books for the
extract from *Rubbish* by Claire Llewellyn, 30; *2wenties* for extract A, 33; Sunworld for
extract B, 33; Penguin Books for extract C from *Spain – the Rough Guide*, 33; © The
Telegraph plc, London, 1995 for the extract from *The Daily Telegraph*, 36, 37; Caters
News Agency Ltd and The Daily Express for the extract from *The Daily Express*, 57;
Woman's Own Magazine for the extract from *Woman's Own*, 60; Bodley Head for the
extract from *Lovers of their Time* by William Trevor, 62; Penguin Books for the extract
from *Cleopatra's Sister* by Penelope Lively (Viking, 1993) copyright © Penelope Lively,
1993, 62; extract from *The Machine Gunners* © Robert Westall 1975, published by
Macmillan Children's Books, 62; Penguin Books for the extract from *Miguel Street* by V
S Naipaul (Penguin Books, 1971) copyright © V S Naipaul, 1959, 65; Margaret Hanbury
Literary Agent for the extracts from *The Gentle Assassin* from the collection *The Day of
Forever* by J G Ballard. Copyright © 1967 by J G Ballard reproduced by permission of
the author c/o Margaret Hanbury, 27 Walcot Square, London SE11 4UB. *The Day of
Forever* is published by Victor Gollancz, London and Flamingo an imprint of
HarperCollins, London, 67; David Higham Associates for the extract from *A Gun for Sale*
by Graham Greene, published by Penguin, 68; Scholastic Publications Ltd for the extract
from *Comfort Herself* by Geraldine Kaye, 70; Orion Publishing Group for the extract
from *The Seige of Krishnapur* by J G Farrell, 71; Penguin Books for the extract from
Dear Nobody by Berlie Doherty (Hamish Hamilton, 1991) copyright © 1991 by Berlie
Doherty, 71; Richard Scott Simon Limited for the extract from *I'm the King of the Castle*
by Susan Hill published by Hamish Hamilton, 72; Casarotto Ramsay Ltd for the extract
from *Countdown* by Alan Ayckbourn, © 1970 by Alan Ayckbourn, page 75 – all rights
whatsoever in this play are strictly reserved and application for performance etc must be
made before rehearsal to Casarotto Ramsay Ltd, National House, 60-66 Wardour Street,
London W1V 4ND, England; Murray Pollinger for the extract from *Heaven's Prisoners*
by James Lee Burke, published by Random Century, London, 77; Routledge & Kegan Paul
for the poem from *Speculations* by T E Hulme, 80; Jonathan Cape for 'Moonlight' by W
H Davies, 80; Penguin Books for the extract of approximately 735 words (pp36–38) from
The Big Sleep by Raymond Chandler (Penguin Books, 1948) copyright © 1939 by

Raymond Chandler, 86, 88; Penguin Books for the extract from *Blood Rights* by Mike
Phillips (Michal Joseph, 1989) copyright © Mike Phillips 1989, 87, 89; Penguin Books
for the extract from *Stone Cold* by Robert Swindells, Hamish Hamilton 1993, text ©
Robert Swindells 1993, 92; Peters Fraser Dunlop for the extract from *Unreliable
Memoirs* by Clive James, 96; Vintage Books for the extract from *A Secret Country* by
John Pilger, 98; Mrs Jean Morgan c/o Campbell Thomson & McLaughlin Ltd for 'Free
Coal' by Robert Morgan; Honno for the extract from *Dangerous Women* by Penny
Windsor, 102; The Portman Group for *Young People and Drinking*, 109; cartoons from
The Punch book of Dogs edited by William Hewson reproduced by permission of Punch,
113; PONT Books for 'Badger' from *Are you talking to me?* by John Tripp (ed)
Jones/Spink, 114; copy advertisement provided by kind permission of Volkswagen Group
United Kingdom Limited t/a Skoda (UK), 124, 125; Today Newspaper for the extract from
Today 9/11/95, 135; HarperCollins *Publishers* Limited for the extract from *The Stories
of Ray Bradbury* by Ray Bradbury (published by Granada in 1983), 140; Kara May for
the extract from *Family Frictions* (Heinemann Floodlights ed. Dan Garrett) by Kara May
© Kara May, 147–150; extract 'A Cream Cracker Under the Settee' from *Talking Heads*
by Alan Bennett reproduced with the permission of the BBC Worldwide Limited, 151;
Macmillan Publishers, Papermac for the extract from 'Tony Kytes the arch-deceiver' from
Collected Short Stories, by Thomas Hardy, 155; Vermilion for the extract from *Growing
up in the 60s* by Cecile Landau, 169; *1st Class*, Wales on Sunday Newspaper for the
extracts, 178, 181.

Every effort has been made to contact the copyright holders. We should be glad to rectify
any omissions at the next reprint if notice is given to the publisher.

The authors would like to thank the following people for their help with this book:

• Adrian Wombwell, shipwright

• Teachers and students at Glyn Derw High School, Cardiff

• Rachel Yeats, Gavin Anderson, Patsy Sterling, K.I.C.K., the people of Kisumu
  Jua Kali, and the staff of VSO, Kisumu

• Staff at VSO, London, especially Silke Bernau

• Tony Farrell and Karen Lewis-Jones for their detailed and helpful assessment
  of the manuscript. All responsibility for the final text is with the authors.

We should like to thank the following for permission to reproduce photographs on the
pages noted:

John Seely 27, 44-48, 127, 175TL/B, 183-191; Holly Stein/Allsport 50, 51; William
Rutten/Pictorial Press Ltd 82L; © Sally and Richard Greenhill 82M; © Clive
Baroa/Performing Arts Library 82BR; David Cannon/Allsport 82TR; Associated
Press/Topham 100; Missouri Historical Society, St Louis 104T/B; Courtesy of Vogue
104M; © Tony Stone Images/Laurie Campbell 114; © RSPCA Photo Library 115;
Barnaby's Picture Library 123TL; DECCA 123TR; D Storey/Barnaby's Picture Library
123T; Barnaby's Picture Library 126TL/BR with Alan Felix; © M D Turner/Barnaby's
Picture Library 126BL; Vernon D Shaw/Popperfoto 126TR; © Syndication International
Ltd 135; The Sun/REX Features 167TL; Brian Rasic/REX Features 167TR; Ammar A8D
Rabbo/REX Features 167MR; Warner Bros 167BR; REX Features 169; Press
Association/Topham 175TR.

Introduction and contents

The Heinemann English Programme 4 is a comprehensive resource for GCSE and Standard Grade. It ensures you will have the skills to approach your exams with confidence and contains lively, imaginative material which we hope you will enjoy using.

Section A introduces and consolidates the skills you require for effective reading, writing and response to literature.

Section B offers longer units for exam practice and coursework.

In the accompanying Teacher's File you will find exam practice papers, mark schemes, and extra differentiated material.

Section A contents

This section introduces and practises the skills you need for effective reading, writing, and response to literature.

An approach to reading

An approach to writing

Forms of writing

Approaching literature

A1 *Reading*

If you want to read well, you need to think about what you are doing.
Ask yourself these questions:

Why am I reading this?

We can read for many different reasons. For example:

- for general information
- to learn how to do something
- to find out a particular fact
- for fun.

What kind of text is this?

It is useful to think about the **kind** of text you are reading and why it was written. Look at these texts. What is each one and why was it written?

It was great to see you and Hannah again after such a long time. And Baby Mark is just the spitting image of his dad! Now we've got together again we mustn't leave it so long before meeting again. I was wondering if you'd like to come over here next time.

6.00 **Home and Away** *(R)* *(309).* *
6.30 **London Tonight** *(361).* *
7.00 **Emmerdale** *(5564).* *
7.30 **Survival.** Conservation-minded farmers explain how they helped stop the decline of the native East Anglian bird, the stone curlew *(S)* *(545).* *
8.00 **The Bill.** Lock up your children, as a five-year-old boy is kidnapped *(4212).* *
8.30 **Blues and Twos.** Police in Chapeltown, Leeds, combat drugs-related crime in this series about the emergency services *(S)* *(4449).* *
9.00 **Thief Takers.** The blatantly ripped-off title sequence and (initially anyway) restless camera-work claim *NYPD Blue* as this British crime drama's spiritual mentor. Beneath the surface, though, it's *The Sweeney* which lives on in this smash-bang-wallop actioner (spotted in pilot form last year) about the work of the Met's Armed Robbery Squad – the Flying Squad to you and me *(9800).* *
10.00 **News, Weather** *(24212).* *
10.30 **Local News,** Weather *(600816).* *

80

Add new life to an old honeysuckle by pruning to just above its base in the spring. Alternatively, cut back older and weaker stems after flowering

Where is everything?

Make sure you look at a text to find out what it contains and where everything is. It may contain information in a number of different forms: words, diagrams, photographs, captions. Make sure you know where they all are and how they link up. Run your eyes over it and find out **where** different information is to be found.

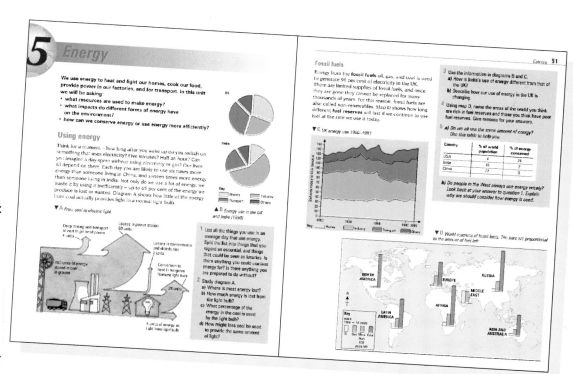

What is it all about?

Before you start reading it in detail, make sure that you know **roughly** what a text is about.

Do I understand it in detail?

Now it is time to read the text carefully and make sure that you understand it in detail. You may not need to read it all; it depends on what you are looking for and why you are reading it. But reading in detail takes time and concentration.

Where to find more information

The next five units are all about reading.

A2 Finding things

explains how to find out answers to:

- 'Where is everything?'
- 'What is it all about?'

and gives you practice.

A3 Same story, different tellers

helps you understand what happens when different writers tell the same story.

A4 Watch out, there's a granny about

gives you practice in reading for detail.

A5 Reading 'between the lines'

Sometimes writers don't spell out what they mean but leave it to you to work things out for yourself. This unit gives you advice about how to do that.

A6 Is that a fact?

When you are reading a newspaper, it is especially important to understand what is a fact and what is just the writer's opinion. This unit shows you how to do that.

A2 *Finding things*

Skimming

When you first look at a text it is very useful to be able to skim. When you skim, you let your eye run over the information and ideas it presents to see:

- what it is about
- where everything is.

With some texts this means skimming pictures as well as words.

What's what

The page opposite contains three kinds of material:

- illustrations
- captions explaining the illustrations
- main text (printed larger).

1 How many illustrations are there?
2 How many captions are there?
3 Are there any illustrations without captions? If so, which?
4 How do you find out which caption belongs to which picture (two answers).
5 How many paragraphs of main text are there?

The pictures and captions

Try to find the answers to these questions quickly, from the pictures and the captions:

1 Who were the first people to use false teeth?
2 Where did ordinary people have their teeth pulled in the Middle Ages?
3 When was the Erado clockwork dentist's drill invented?
4 Which university developed an implant for stopping tooth decay?
5 Who first tried to use anaesthetic when extracting teeth?

Words and meanings

The words in column **A** are all in the captions. Column **B** contains their meanings – but they are jumbled. Can you work out which meaning goes with each word?

A	B
antibiotic	something that is placed in the body for a period of time as a medical treatment
anaesthetic	a coating that forms on your teeth and can cause dental problems
plaque	a medical substance used to destroy harmful organisms in the body
implant	something which kills pain

DENTISTRY

△ FALSE TEETH were used as early as 700 BC by the Etruscan people. They used human or animal teeth and bound them to real teeth with gold wire.

DENTISTRY did not become a profession until the 19th century. Some ancient civilisations such as the Etruscans made simple dentures, but until anaesthetics were first used in the 1850s, rotten teeth were removed with pliers with no attempt to lessen the pain. Tooth decay was widespread. Wealthy Europeans were eating so much sugar in the 16th century that their teeth turned black.

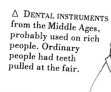

△ DENTAL INSTRUMENTS from the Middle Ages, probably used on rich people. Ordinary people had teeth pulled at the fair.

▽ 19TH-CENTURY DENTURES made of human teeth, gold and ivory.

△ HORACE WELLS tried to extract a tooth painlessly using anaesthetic, but his patient groaned and the spectators were unconvinced.

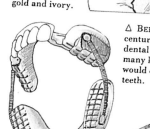

△ BEFORE the 19th century there was no dental profession, so many kinds of people would offer to pull out teeth.

In the 150 years since anaesthetics were first used in dentistry, the techniques and equipment involved have improved greatly. Today dentists can even put back a tooth that has been knocked out accidentally. Techniques have been invented to stop teeth from decaying, to whiten them and to straighten them. Today it is difficult to tell whether people have dentures or not.

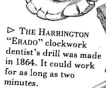

▷ THE HARRINGTON "ERADO" clockwork dentist's drill was made in 1864. It could work for as long as two minutes.

GUM DISEASE can be treated with an acrylic strip containing an antibiotic (*right*).

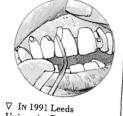

▽ IN 1991 Leeds University Dental Health Department developed a fluoride-releasing implant that will prevent teeth from decaying.

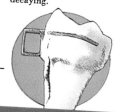

◁ △ A DENTIST'S SURGERY in the 1930s (*left*) looked different from one today (*above*). Dentists now have access to increasingly sophisticated equipment such as ultrasound probes, which use high frequency sound waves to break up plaque.

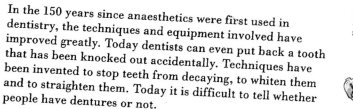

25

The main text

Read the text below which is a copy of the main text from page 9. Try to find the answers to these questions quickly:

1 Roughly how long ago were anaesthetics first used by dentists?
2 The text uses another word for 'false teeth'. What is it?
3 When did being a dentist first become a proper job?
4 What made rich people's teeth turn black in the sixteenth century?
5 The writer lists four things modern dentists can do. What are they?

DENTISTRY did not become a profession until the 19th century. Some ancient civilisations such as the Etruscans made simple dentures, but until anaesthetics were first used in the 1850s, rotten teeth were
5 removed with pliers with no attempt to lessen the pain. Tooth decay was widespread. Wealthy Europeans were eating so much sugar in the 16th century that their teeth turned black.

In the 150 years since anaesthetics were first used in
10 dentistry, the techniques and equipment involved have improved greatly. Today dentists can even put back a tooth that has been knocked out accidentally. Techniques have been invented to stop teeth from decaying, to whiten them and to straighten them. Today it is difficult to tell whether
15 people have dentures or not.

From the Timelines series: *Medicine*

A3 *Same story, different tellers*

Looking at how information is presented

The same information can be presented in different ways. Different writers will arrange their ideas in a different order and select different aspects of the subject to emphasise.

Sometimes it is obvious why two writers tell the same story in different ways. Look at these two reports of a football match.

A

HILLSIDE WIN AGAIN

IN A BRUISING ENCOUNTER with local rivals, Park Town, Hillside notched up yet another victory, defeating their visitors 2-1 in a closely-contested game.

A fluke shot put Park Town one up in the seventeenth minute, but Hillside mounted a relentless attack to produce a well-deserved equaliser just before half-time.

Much of the second half saw Park Town camped in the Hillside half, but to no avail. Resolute defending by the home team frustrated all their attempts to take the lead. At last, despite losing their captain midway through the half, Hillside counter-attacked and snatched a winning goal only seconds before the final whistle.

B

Dirty game ends in defeat

YET AGAIN local rivals Hillside showed their determination to win at any cost, when Park Town visited them last week. An early goal by Park Town laid the foundation for a long period of domination by the visitors. Unfortunately a barrage of fouls and doubtful decisions by the referee allowed the home side to score an equaliser.

For much of the second half Park Town mounted attack after attack on the Hillside goal. But they were met with vicious and sometimes dangerous tackling. The Hillside skipper was sent off for dangerous play, but only after two Park Town players had been forced off the field by injury. Seriously weakened, Park Town conceded a lucky goal to their opponents well into injury time.

Questions

1 Which side was each writer supporting?
2 Explain why you think this. Give the line numbers of the parts which make you think so.
3 Does report **A** contain any facts that report **B** misses out?
4 Does report **B** contain any facts that report **A** misses out?

5 What parts of the match does report **A** emphasise?
6 What parts of the match does report **B** emphasise?
7 Why does report **A** not explain why Hillside lost their captain?

The Heinemann English Programme 4 – Foundation

11

A story about Herakles

Some stories are told and retold time after time. The stories that follow both describe one of the adventures of the Greek hero Herakles, half man and half god. To pay for a terrible crime he had committed, Herakles was told by the gods that he must go and serve King Eurystheus for twelve years and perform a number of heroic tasks set by the king. These were the 'Labours of Herakles'.

Read the stories and then follow the instructions that follow them.

A

King Eurystheus was clever and cocky, but he was also as timid as a mouse. When he looked up at Herakles, his stomach churned and turned right over.

'Twelve years is it?' said the king. 'I must set you labours that are
5   worth your while. First ... bring me the lion of Nemea.'

Herakles found the lion at the entrance to the cave. His chops were streaky with dark human blood. Herakles shot eagle-feathered arrows at him, but the arrows bounced off the lion's thick skin. Then he shouted and slammed his club down on to the lion's skull. The lion just frowned, and
10   blinked, and lolloped into his cave.

Bones! Feathers! Fur! Hair! The air inside the cave was thick and sour.

Herakles grabbed the lion by his mane and the beast raised one paw and swatted him. Then the man-god and the king of the beasts wrestled and roared. The lion bit off one of Herakles' fingers, and Herakles,
15   enraged, locked the lion's head under his right arm; he squeezed until the lion choked to death.

Herakles used the beast's own razor claws to cut through his tough skin, and carried the pelt back to Mycenae.

'I'll wear this pelt,' he told King Eurystheus. 'From this day on the lion's
20   strength will be my strength.'

Eurystheus had supposed the lion would eat Herakles for his midday meal. He was so afraid of his servant that he forbade him to step inside the city walls again.

Kevin Crossley-Holland: *The labours of Herakles*

pelt: *animal skin*

B

Eurystheus first sent Herakles to skin the Nemean lion. Selene the moon-goddess
had created this monster: she moulded sea-foam into a lion's shape, and breathed
life into it. Its claws were razors; its skin was weapon-proof. It ate human flesh, and
had killed or frightened away the local people for miles around. It took Herakles
5   thirty days to track the lion to its mountain lair. The monster had recently killed,
and was sleepy after its meal, or it would never have let Herakles near. He clubbed
it hard – not on its weapon-proof skin but on the end of its nose. The lion sneezed
in surprise and backed into its cave. Herakles ran in after it and strangled it. He
skinned it with its own razor-claws – the only things sharp enough to cut the hide –
10 flung the skin round his shoulders and made a cap from its gaping jaws. Then he
shouldered his club and went back to Mycenae. Eurystheus' servants told their
master that Herakles was walking up the slope to the Lion Gate, and wearing the
lion – and Eurystheus (who had never expected to see him alive again) completely
lost his nerve. He buried a huge bronze jar in a hole in the ground; then he climbed
15 inside and hid, trembling, until the royal steward gave Herakles his next task and
Herakles went away.

Kenneth McLeish: *Children of the gods*

Who says?

Read the statements in the table below. For each one put a
tick in the correct box. The first one has been done for you.

Statement	This information is found:		
	In both stories	Only in A	Only in B
Eurystheus asked Herakles to bring him the lion's *skin*.			✔
When Herakles arrived he saw the lion by the entrance to the cave.			
When Herakles arrived the lion was sleepy.			
Herakles shot at the lion.			
Herakles clubbed it on the end of its nose.			
It sneezed.			
It blinked.			
It bit off Herakles' finger.			
Herakles wrestled with it.			

Now make up a similar table for the rest of the story.
You should be able to make at least five more statements.

A4 Watch out, there's a granny about

Reading in detail

There are many situations in life where it is important to read carefully and take in all the details of a text – your life may even depend on it. After a first reading to 'get your bearings', read slowly and make sure that your eye is not skipping important information. If necessary read the text several times.

Over the last six months, six of my friends in London have been physically assaulted: in all cases without warning and, in every
5 case bar one, by a complete stranger. One girl was left with large chunks of hair torn out and impressive gouges across her face and neck; one man was
10 beaten so hard that he had raised welts across his back under four layers of clothing afterwards. The others escaped with mild shock and bruising.
15 They were all under 30, and they had all been attacked by old age pensioners.

impressive: that would immediately catch your attention
gouges: deép scratches
welts: bruises that have swollen up

Questions

1 Is each of these statements true or false?

  a The attacks averaged one per week.
  b All the attacks were made by older people on younger people.
  c All the attackers knew their victims.

2 How many of the victims were injured?
3 One of the victims was badly injured on the back. What else do we learn about this person?
4 One girl was attacked. What were her injuries?

Now read the rest of the article and answer the questions at the end.

Natasha, a lawyer, was coming out of a supermarket when an old man turned round and began hitting her with his walking-stick. She ended up having to run away. David had also been hit, repeatedly and very hard, with a walking-stick, after an elderly woman had stepped out in front of his motorbike without waiting for the traffic lights. It was sheer luck, he said, that he didn't kill her; she obviously disagreed. James had been standing, quite innocently, next to a short, pugnacious old man on the tube. He'd begun muttering to himself about the youth of today before suddenly thumping James (28) around the head.

Clare, a BBC director, had brushed against a heavily jewelled, fat old woman at the theatre. 'I apologised,' she said. 'And basically this woman shoved me up against the seat and started punching me.' Much the same thing had happened to Victoria in a cinema. Sarah, unusually, had actually known her attacker, her 75-year-old neighbour. 'You bastard, you bastard,' she was screaming, as she clawed at Sarah's face. 'I'll get you.' They had had a minor disagreement about a door lock a few days earlier; it was the closest any of the attacks came to having a reason.

Few people of my age can understand why we should always forgive old people's rudeness, their intolerance, their apparently miraculous ability to be hobbling down a street one minute and galloping towards a free bus seat with the speed of a turbo-charged Zimmer frame the next. Legally, they get to play by an entirely different set of rules, as Sarah, the one person who reported being attacked by an OAP, found out. The police, who hardly smirked at all, agreed she had a case, but advised her to drop it. 'Let's face it, love,' they told her, 'no court's going to convict an old granny, no matter what she's done.' Just because there are only a handful of pensioners currently in prison does not mean that more don't deserve to be. 'In all seriousness,' agreed a Police Federation spokesman, 'we could be looking at a real problem here. If old people think they can get away with it, we're in danger of sending the wrong message.'

The Spectator

Questions

1 The first two paragraphs on this page give details of several attacks.
Make up a table like this, containing all the information given.

Victim	Attacker	Place	Other information
Natasha	old man	outside supermarket	he used a stick

2 Which attacks were similar to each other and why?
3 How many victims complained to the police?
4 What advice did the police give?
5 The Police Federation spokesman said, 'we could be looking at a real problem here.' What did he mean?

A5 Reading 'between the lines'

When you write something, the words you put on the page are only a small part of what you are thinking. They are the 'tip of the iceberg'. Sometimes a writer works very hard to make very clear what they have in mind. At other times they may decide to leave it to the reader to work out what is going on.

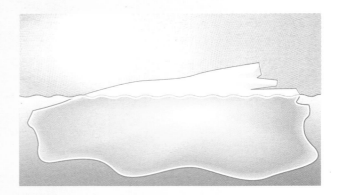

Working out the story

The poem on the opposite page takes the form of a conversation. As we read we have to try to work out the story behind the conversation.

1 Who is the first speaker?
2 What is the first thing she asks?
3 Who is the second speaker?
4 What is his answer?
5 What does he ask his mother to do and why?
6 What new information do we learn in the second verse?
7 Verses 3 and 4 give us two new pieces of information. If you put them together, do they suggest what may have happened?
8 The last verse gives us an idea of **what** has happened, but it does not explain **why** or **how**. What do you think may be the answers to these questions and what makes you think so:
   ■ Was the poisoning accidental or deliberate?
   ■ What part did his true love play in the tragedy?
   ■ Why is the last line of the last verse different from the last lines of all the other verses?

Telling the story

Think about your answers to the questions and work out a full version of what happened in the story behind the conversation. Tell the 'real story' to the rest of your group or the rest of your class.

Lord Randal

'O where have you been, Lord Randal, my son?
O where have you been, my handsome young man?'
'I have been to the wild wood; mother make my bed soon.
For I'm weary with hunting, and fain would lie down.'

5 'Where got you your dinner, Lord Randal, my son?
Where got you your dinner, my handsome young man?'
'I dined with my true-love; mother, make my bed soon,
For I'm weary with hunting and fain would lie down.'

'What had you for your dinner, Lord Randal, my son?
10 What had you for your dinner, my handsome young man?'
'I had eels boiled in broth; mother, make my bed soon,
For I'm weary with hunting and fain would lie down.'

'What became of your bloodhounds, Lord Randal, my son?
What became of your bloodhounds, my handsome young man?'
15 'O they swelled and they died; mother, make my bed soon,
For I'm weary with hunting and fain would lie down.'

'O I fear you are poisoned, Lord Randal, my son?
O I fear you are poisoned, my handsome young man?'
'O yes! I am poisoned; mother, make my bed soon,
20 For I'm sick at the heart and fain would lie down.'

Anon

fain would: want to

The start of a story

We have to work particularly hard when we read the opening of a story.

> 'Dad? Dad! It's Eve. How are you? What are you doing with yourself? Are you all right?'
>
> 'Eve? Eve darling, how are you? God, it's good to hear your voice. Where are you? ...

It's a daughter talking to her father.

They haven't seen each other for some time.

They aren't in the same place, so they must be talking by phone or radio.

What can you work out from the next few sentences of the story? Use the prompt questions to guide your thoughts.

5 ... Why can't I see you?'
Eve smiled happily. It was so good to hear if not see her Dad again. Somehow it made the idea of returning home seem closer and more real. 'Dad, the screen of this video-phone isn't
10 working. And the fleet's just returned to Tdir-ah so the queues to use the phones are *ginormous*. It was use this phone or wait for another week to find a phone with a working screen.'
'No, no, it's enough just hearing your voice,
15 bunny. Are you all right?'
'I'm fine Dad.' Eve smiled again, stretching out a tentative arm to the blank screen before her. 'I've missed you so much. I just can't wait to get home.'
20 'So the reports are true? The war *is* finally over?'

Malorie Blackman: *Not so stupid!*

- Why should he expect to be able to 'see' her, when they are using a telephone?

- Why is she away from home? And how long has she been away for?
- 'Fleet' of what?
- What kind of place-name is Tdir-ah? So what kind of place might it be?

- What can you work out about the time and place in which the story is set?

- What extra information do we learn from the last sentence?

After school

Now read this story extract and work out as much as you can from it. Again, use the prompt questions to guide your thoughts, but read the extract all through once first.

On a sharp autumn evening a boy stood waiting inside the high stone pillars which flanked the gateway of the Jones Academy for the Sons of Gentlemen and Respectable Tradesmen in the small town of Pennygaff.

School had finished for the day some time since, and all the other scholars had gladly streamed away into the windy dusk, but still the boy hesitated, shivering with cold and indecision. Once or twice he edged close against one of the soot-blackened pillars, so that his form was almost invisible, and, leaning forward, peered out through the close-set iron railings.

The street outside seemed empty. But was it really so? Very little daylight now remained. A thin yellow strip of light in the west made the shadows along the narrow cobbled way even blacker; there were too many doorways, porches, passages, and flights of steps in or behind which any number of enemies could lurk unseen. And a great bank of purple-black cloud was advancing steadily westward across the sky, blotting out what little light yet lingered. In a minute, torrents of rain would fall.

The sound of quick footsteps behind him rang in the paved yard and the boy swung round sharply, but it was only the schoolmaster, Mr Price, on his way home to tea.

Joan Aiken: *The whispering mountain*

Based on what you have read so far, what do you think will happen next and why?

- Where and when does this story take place?

- Why is he alone?

- What is he waiting for?
- Is he hiding from something?

- This shows us what he sees. Does it give us any clues about the answers to the previous two questions?

- Why does he swing round 'sharply'?

A6 *Is that a fact?*

Fact and opinion

An **opinion** is an expression of a personal belief. For example:

Glasgow has a better shopping centre than Edinburgh.

You cannot prove that Glasgow is better in such a way that everyone will agree with you; different people will have different views.
A **fact** is a statement that can be **shown** to be true. For example:

Edinburgh is the capital city of Scotland.

Statements of fact can be *true* or *false*. Opinions cannot be true or false – you can either agree with them or disagree with them.

Title

Look at the two pictures below. Then read the statements opposite. Decide whether each statement is:

a ✔ a true factual statement

b ✘ a false factual statement

c 👍 an opinion you agree with

d 👎 an opinion you disagree with.

1 Julian is better-looking than Chris.
2 Chris is taller than Julian.
3 Julian's car is grey.
4 Julian's car is a sports car.
5 Chris's car is a saloon car.
6 Chris's car is an old banger.
7 Chris lives in a flat.
8 Julian lives in a better house than Chris.
9 Chris is not as well-off as Julian.
10 Julian likes gardening.

Julian

Chris

What the papers say

Newspapers contain a mixture of fact and opinion. Often they don't agree in their interpretation of the news. Here are two headlines and photographs from the day when a famous tennis player lost a valuable sponsorship contract.

Steffi, laughing off a $1m loss

Desolate Graf talks of ordeal

In the box below are several short cuttings from newspapers. Some are statements of fact and some are expressions of opinion. Which is which?

BRAVEST MAN OF THE YEAR

TV bosses' square meal is humbug

A PENSIONER was arrested after driving for 14 miles the wrong way along a motorway with only three wheels on his car.

COURT THREAT OVER £0 BILL

STUDENT David Lavin was threatened with legal action – for owing British Gas absolutely NOTHING.

David, 20, of Newport, Gwent, was billed for £0.00 – and told he would be taken to court if he didn't pay. The firm later apologised.

THE WORST floods in living memory left the Isle of Wight on the brink of catastrophe last night.

'Fact is sacred'

Traditionally the 'news' pages contain facts and the 'opinion' columns contain opinions.

Fact

Mum and girl die as blaze wrecks home

A mother and her two-year-old daughter died yesterday when fire swept through the upper storey of their home.

The woman's husband escaped by leaping through a bedroom window before forcing his way back through a rear door to rescue their two other daughters, both aged under eight.

He was taken to the West Wales General Hospital and detained for treatment for cuts and burns. The two rescued children were taken to hospital for observation but were not hurt.

The Birmingham Post

Opinion

Will the Royal Family ever learn? Instead of doing something to repair its tattered image, Prince Charles spent Boxing Day showing Prince Harry how to shoot pheasants at point-blank range.

Perhaps Charles's advisers have never told him that the vast majority of the British public does not like to see wildlife slaughtered for fun.

Yet again, the Royals have shot themselves in the foot.

Daily Mirror

Quite often, however, popular newspapers combine fact and opinion and present it as 'news'.

Blast for teachers

OPINION — **Loudmouth** **Leftie teachers who mobbed**
FACT — **blind** **MP David Blunkett are off the hook.**
OPINION — The rabble-rousers will not be punished and are back in the classroom, it was revealed yesterday. — FACT — FACT

And they haven't even apologised for their brutal actions at the NUT conference in Blackpool last month. — OPINION

Angry Mr Blunkett, Labour's education spokesman, said: 'How can they command respect in the classroom now and undo the damage they've done their profession?'

It's a FACT that he said it, but he's expressing his OPINION

The Star

Which is which?

This newspaper extract contains a similar mixture of fact and opinion. Read it carefully and then follow the instructions in **What to do**.

We send in the girls

Tears and pride as women soldiers join lads in Bosnia battle zone hell

Three brave Army girls were last night helping to spearhead the massive airlift to save Our Boys in Bosnia. 5

Lance-Corporal Susan Taylor and Signaller Tracy Farr boarded a Hercules yesterday to fly out with a squad of male comrades. 10

And Corporal Tracey Duggan was on standby waiting to join them with her own unit, the fearsome 24 Air-mobile Brigade.

Susan, 21, and Tracy, 24, both of 30 Signals, left RAF Lyneham in Wiltshire for the Croatian port of Split. 15

For blonde Tracy the order to go brought joy – for it will reunite her with her soldier boyfriend.

Corporal John Poole, 27, who is also in 30 Signals, was flown out with an earlier detachment five weeks ago. The couple began dating when Tracy returned to Britain from 20 a year-long stint in Wildenrath, Germany.

They vowed to wait for each other when John was sent off with an advance party of the regiment, based in Nuneaton, Warwicks.

The Sun

What to do

1 Copy out the table at the bottom of the page.
2 Read the article again and find at least five more statements of fact.
3 Write each one in the table.
4 Read the article again and this time find at least two more expressions of opinion.
5 Write these in the table.

	Statements of fact	Expressions of opinion
1	Women soldiers have been sent to Bosnia.	Life in the battle zone is 'hell'.
2		
3		
4		
5		
6		

A7 *Approaching writing*

Successful writing is more complicated than just sitting down and writing whatever comes into your head. There are three main stages.

1 Getting ready

2 Drafting

3 Presentation

Getting ready

■ Think carefully about the writing task. ➤ Make sure that you have a clear idea of:

■ the **audience** you are writing for (see unit A9 on page 28)
■ **why** you are writing (see unit A8 on page 26)
■ exactly **what** you are writing about.

■ Collect ideas and information.

■ Plan what you are going to write. ➤ ■ If you are only writing a short piece you may be able to plan it in your head. Usually it is better to write your plan down.

Drafting

■ Write a first draft.

■ If possible get someone else to read and comment on your first draft.

■ Read over your work yourself.

■ Re-write the first draft to improve it. ➤ You may be able to do this by changing the first draft. You may have to start all over again. It depends.

■ Check the final version for mistakes. ➤ Look for mistakes in the:

■ spelling
■ punctuation
■ grammar.

Presentation

■ Plan the layout of the page(s).
■ Prepare any pictures or diagrams.
■ Write or word-process the final version.

A8 Why write?

Purposes for writing

Whenever we write we have one or more purposes. The commonest of these are:

Purpose	Examples
■ to tell people things	newspapers, factual books
■ to persuade people to do or think something	advertisements
■ to tell people what to do	laws, rules, instructions
■ to 'get on with' people	personal letters
■ to entertain	novels, comics
■ to keep a record of things.	diaries

So what are these?

Read these short texts and say what you think the purposes are.

A

Cut a dash to
FRANCE

Step out in style this summer aboard the elegant
SeaCat. It's in a class of its own as it glides effortlessly
between Folkestone and Boulogne in just 55 minutes.

The twin hulled catamaran's striking
good looks are perfectly complemented with a
tastefully appointed interior. Relax in the spacious and
modern surroundings, ordering drinks and duty free
goods from the comfort of your seat – or take in the
air on the outer deck.

B

REMEMBER: if you sell or pass this
vehicle to someone else

● You must fill in the 'notification of
Sale or Transfer' slip overleaf and
send it to DVLC yourself to show that
you are no longer responsible for
this vehicle or its use.

C

'Sit down, young man,' said the
Official.
'Thanks.' The young man sat.
'I've been hearing rumours about
you,' the Official said pleasantly. 'Oh,
nothing much. Your nervousness. Your
not getting on so well. Several months
now I've heard about you, and I
thought I'd call you in. Thought maybe
you'd like your job changed. Like to go
overseas, work in some other War
Area? Desk job killing you off, like to
get right in on the old fight?'
'I don't think so,' said the young
sergeant.

D

7.00	Top of the Pops (T) (S) *7035*	
7.30	EastEnders (T) (S) *734*	
8.00	Zoo Watch Live (S) *6783*	
8.30	Agony Again (T) *5290*	

Your turn

Look at the picture and captions and then follow the instructions in **What to do**.

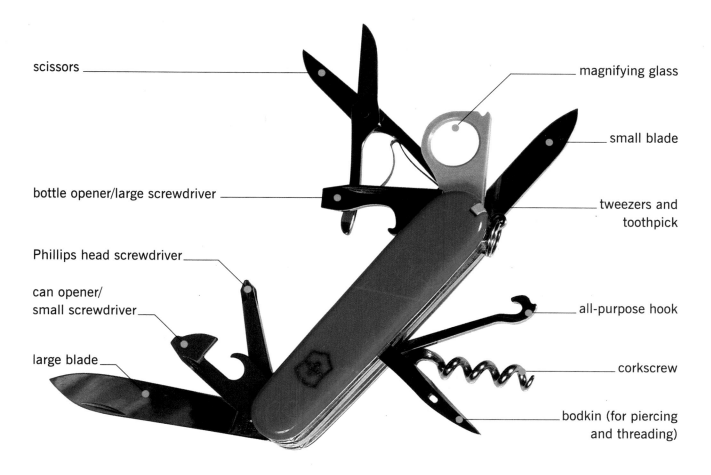

scissors

magnifying glass

small blade

bottle opener/large screwdriver

tweezers and toothpick

Phillips head screwdriver

can opener/
small screwdriver

all-purpose hook

large blade

corkscrew

bodkin (for piercing
and threading)

What to do

You are going to base two pieces of writing on an object. You can
use the penknife in the picture, or anything similar that you know well.

1

You want to buy a present for a friend. You
think this penknife would be a good present,
but you are not sure that your friend would
like it. You decide to ask another friend if
they think it would be a good present.
You **describe** the penknife so that they have
a clear idea of what it is like. Write what
you would say.

2

Christmas is coming and you have been
given the job of advertising this penknife.
The photograph above will be used in a
magazine advertisement. Write the words
to go with it. Remember that you have to
persuade people that this penknife is a
brilliant idea for a present.

The Heinemann English Programme 4 – Foundation

A9 *Who's it for?*

Thinking of your audience

When you write for someone else they must find your writing easy to understand. Writers have to think about the needs of their audience. They have to ask themselves:

- how well can my audience use English?
- how well can they read?
- how much do they know about the subject?

Words

Some words are easier to read and understand than others. If a piece of writing contains too many hard words it will be difficult to understand. Look at this group of words:

debris   cast-off   flotsam   **dross**   refuse   spoilage

clinker   *cullet*   **jetsam**   jumble   **trash**   litter

bilge   rubbish   lumber   junk   rejects   **waste**

1 Write the words down in two lists:

  A words you know the meaning of
  B words you have not come across before.

2 Use a dictionary to find out the meanings of the words in list B.
3 Look at list A and underline the five words that you think are easiest to understand – the kind of words you could use when talking to a young child.

Sentences

Now look at these three sentences:

A The public is encouraged to separate paper and glass for recycling and to avoid throwing away high-hazard items with the domestic waste.
B Sort your rubbish before you throw it away. Collect paper and glass for recycling. Do not throw dangerous things away with ordinary rubbish.
C People should collect paper and glass for recycling and should not throw away dangerous things with household rubbish.

Which is the easiest to understand and which is the hardest? Why?
Think about:

- the words
- how long the sentences are
- how complicated the sentences are
- the punctuation.

When you write for a particular audience you need to think carefully about:

- the words you use and how difficult they are
- how long and complicated your sentences are.

Reading about rubbish

Read this text and then answer the questions beside it:

A

> Not all of our rubbish needs to be thrown away. Some of it can be used again – like the empty milk bottles people put on the doorstep each day.
> 5 Some of our rubbish can't be used again, but it can help to make new materials. This is called recycling.
> Do you know of any materials that can be recycled?

Nigel Hawkes: *Toxic waste and recycling*

Questions

1 This text has been written for young children. What age do you think it is suitable for?
2 Are there any difficult words in it? If so, which are they?
3 Are the difficult words properly explained?
4 Are there any sentences that are too long or too complicated? If so, which ones?

Now read this text and answer the same questions about it.

B

> The industrial world is also realising that many waste materials are too valuable to throw away. Old cars are 'cannibalised' for spare parts in scrap yards, then melted down as scrap which goes to make steel for another generation of cars. Some glass
> 5 bottles can be used up to thirty times if they are collected and cleaned. Broken glass – 'cullet' – can be recycled to make new bottles, saving raw materials and energy. Waste paper can also be used again. In 1984, paper recycling programmes in nine industrial countries spared a million acres of trees. Recycling
> 10 aluminium drink cans requires only a twentieth as much energy as making fresh aluminium from bauxite ore.

Claire Llewellyn: *Rubbish*

The rewrite

Extract **B** is much more difficult than extract **A**. But the ideas and information in it **can** be explained to young children if the right language is used.

Sorting out the information

1 Read extract **B** again. Make a list of the main ideas in it, like this:

- waste materials valuable
- <u>old cars</u> – spare parts
  - – melted down for steel for new cars
- <u>bottles</u> –

Thinking about the words

2 Now look at the notes you have made.
3 Find any words that you think are difficult and need to be explained. Make a list of them.
4 Next to each one write an explanation that your readers will understand.

Writing the sentences

5 Now write a text which contains all the information in your notes **and** the explanations of the difficult words. Try to write short sentences and make sure that they are correctly punctuated. For example you could start like this:

People now understand that much of our rubbish is valuable. We can use it again instead of throwing it away

Checking

Work with a partner.

6 Show your writing to your partner.
7 Comment on each other's work and suggest how the writing could be improved.

Final version

8 Now write a final version, making any changes you have agreed with your partner.

A10 *It depends if I know them or not*

Tone and formality

The **way** in which we address other people – in speech or writing – is called **tone**. It is made up of:

- the words we use
- the way in which we construct our sentences
- (if we are speaking) the way in which we pronounce words and sentences.

If we are addressing someone we do not know we are more likely to use more **formal** language. With friends we are more likely to be **informal**.

Role play

Work with a partner.

1 Look at the top picture and decide what you think is going on.
2 Decide who will play **A** and who will play the friend.
3 Decide how the conversation begins.
4 When you are both ready, act out the conversation between the two people.
5 When you have finished, do the same with the bottom picture, with the same person as **A** and the other as the householder.

Discussion

After you have finished the second conversation, discuss:

1 How did **A** change their:
   - behaviour?
   - language?
   - way of speaking?
   between the two conversations.
2 Were these changes true to life? If not, how could they have been improved?

The Heinemann English Programme 4 – Foundation

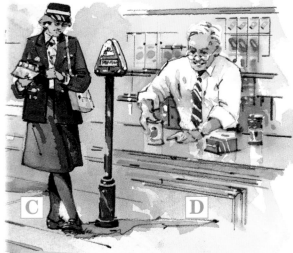

Greetings!

1 Different people greet their friends in different ways. Look at the people in the picture. How do you think each of them would speak to a friend they know well? Choose one of the greetings from the box or use one you have thought of yourself.

2 We also often use different greetings when speaking to people we do not know. How do you think each of the people above would greet a stranger?

Hi!
How do you do?
How're you doing?
All right?
How's tricks?
Hallo.
Long time no see.
Look what the cat's brought in.
Good morning.

Help!

For the questions that follow, imagine that:

- you know **A** very well – you are friends
- **B** is a complete stranger whom you have never seen before in your life
- you have seen **C** once or twice before but have never spoken to her
- **D** owns a small shop near you and knows you and your family because you are regular customers.

What would you say to each of the four in these situations?

1 You have been speaking to them and you want to say goodbye.
2 You want to thank them for helping you.
3 You want to find out the way to somewhere.
4 You want advice on the time of a bus or train.

Why?

1 In what ways would you speak differently to those four people?
2 Why should we speak in different ways to different people?
3 How do we know how we should speak to different people?

Different readers

Just as we use a different tone when we speak to different people, so we also write in different ways according to our audience. Look at these three texts and then answer the questions that follow.

A

The 'White Coast' is
white HOT!

It's one of the most buzzing strips for an excellent holiday. Miles of white sandy beaches combined with one of Europe's best sunshine records. 2wentys always stay where the action 'thumps' and that's right slap bang on the coast in Benidorm – the wildest of all the Costa Blanca resorts ... As the temperature is HOT, bronzing that body will be a breeze. Clear waters, beautiful beaches and non-stop party nights are what its all about back in Benidorm. 5 10 15

B

With the best year round climate in Spain, the 'White Coast' has been at the forefront of the expansion in overseas home ownership for discerning British and other Europeans. Resorts with fine long Beaches like Calpe and Denia have become spacious modern townships without losing their identity to high-rise hotel development. 5

C

South of Valencia stretches a long strip of country with some of the best beaches on this coast, especially between Gandía and Benidorm. Much of it, though, suffers from the worst excesses of package tourism and in summer it's hard to get a room anywhere – in August it's virtually impossible. Campers have it somewhat 5 easier – there are hundreds of campsites – but driving can be a nightmare unless you stick to the dull highway.

1 **A** and **B** are both selling holidays. What kind of customers do you think each wants to attract?
2 What makes you think this?
3 **C** provides information. What kind of audience do you think the text is aimed at?
4 What makes you think this?

Writing

1 Think of a place in this country that would appeal to the audience for **A**. Imagine that you are trying to 'sell' it to them. Write a paragraph explaining why it is **just** the place for them.

2 Now do the same for **B**, choosing a different place.
3 Choose one of the two places you have written about. Write a brief description of it for the readers of **C**.

A11 Making notes: why?

---

specific heat capacity test.   15 June

We did this simple experiment to find out the specific heat capacity of different materials. This is what we used:

Equipment:

Matt,
Thermometer,
Heating eliment,
power pack (50 watt),
1k of :   Al,
         Cu,
         Fe,
         Brass,
         H_2O,

Small quantity of oil
Stop clock,

The   masses of metals all had holes in for the and   thermometers. setup like this:

— Wires to powerpack
ng eliment

Janet

Tanya phone from holiday asked where you were, not out with other girls she hoped! she said hi and she'll phone tomorrow at 6.00pm

Rob

Burning coal - Sulphur dioxide

Chimney from boiler, nitrogen oxides =

Cooling Towers - steam.

lime on lakes ~~very~~ expensive.

sulphur has been scrubbed out   **expensive**

nitrogen oxides from cars.
80% of

INT. WITH 'J.E.' - Worker @ a Youth Centre for teens.

How did you get involved?   Why?
- Boredom! Summer hols. Likes/relates to kids. friend already working.

Benefits (kids)? What makes them come?
- Fun! Warm/friendly atmosphere
- Approachable people
- Local
- Inexpensive

Actvities?
- Anything!
   - Sports, social events - fun & serious (ie. Low key drugs talks)
- Trips - 'Gladiators', discos, skating

High spots.
- ~~Boy/job/wage~~, - watching changes
- "Thank you" card, from one of the kids.

---

shopping
present for Janice
birthday card for John
noterlets

fruit & veg
orange juice
milk

Radio Times

---

explain how acid rain travels from one country to another?

Prevailing winds ←
from tall chimneys & u.   a travels
to sweden and Norway.

What can ~~be~~ done to reduce the problem?
spread lime on lake to reduce the acidity for a short time
talking sulphur out of coal when its burning. but its very expensive process.

What and why?

For each piece of writing on page 34, decide:

- who might have written it
- who it was written for
- why it might have been written.

Do the texts have anything in common?

Discussion

You are often asked to write notes in school.

1 What is meant by the word 'notes'?
2 How do you make notes?
3 Why do you make notes?
4 Do the answers to these questions change according to the teacher
   or the school subject?

Research

Think back over the past five school days: how many times have you
made notes? Make up a table like the one below. Include all the note-
writing you have done, including any you did just for yourself – without
being asked to by a teacher.

Subject	What the notes were about	What they were for	Comments
History	Cuban missile crisis	to help us learn and remember what the book said	the teacher set the notes for homework and checked them afterwards
English	Factory farming	to remember what our group decided, so we could tell the rest of the class	the teacher told us to make notes – but it didn't matter what they looked like as long as we could understand them

A12 Making notes: how?

Winning smile of a girl called Jaws

A teenager picked on by school bullies because she had buck teeth has landed a leading role in a television commercial for toothpaste.

Simone McGregor became the butt of jokes by classmates when her
5 front teeth began to protrude over her bottom lip from the age of nine. She became so self-conscious that she found it hard to look anyone in the face, let alone pose for the camera.

Simone, now 17, of Llanelli, Dyfed, was talking with friends in the playground when a girl shouted at her: 'You've got the worst teeth I've
10 ever seen.'

She said: 'Someone else said I looked like Bugs Bunny and the whole group fell about laughing.'

Cut out little words like 'is' and 'and'

Mark off the **main points** in some way:

- underlining
- different colour highlighter

Simone McGregor – 17 – lives in Llanelli

Just landed role in television toothpaste commercial

Bullied at school because of buck teeth

- started when aged 9
- girl shouted, 'You've got the worst teeth I've ever seen.'
- told she looked 'like Bugs Bunny'
- all laughed at her

Use plenty of space

Group together things that belong together

Experiment

Now do this experiment to see how well you can make notes.
Follow these instructions exactly.

1 Below is the rest of the story. Read it carefully, and make notes on it. Allow no more than five minutes to do this.
2 After five minutes, close the book.
3 Use your notes to retell the story in as much detail as you can.
4 Open the book again and check your version against the original.
5 Underneath your version, write down any important details you have missed out.

'Over the next couple of years I lost all my self-esteem. Breaks and lunchtimes were always the worst for teasing. Someone would ask me if I wanted a carrot and more and more people would join in.'

When she was 11, Simone was fitted with a metal brace, and had eight teeth extracted to help straighten her smile. The taunts started again when she wore the brace, with new nicknames such as 'Jaws' and 'Metal Mouth'. Simone later plucked up courage to appear in a charity clothes show. She was then signed up by the London-based model agency NEW and at 15 appeared on the catwalk in Tokyo. Two months ago she was filmed for the television advertisement.

She said: 'It seemed almost comical that my teeth had helped me to get the work so quickly. My confidence soared.'

The Daily Telegraph

Summing up

An important way we use writing in school is to help us remember things, by making notes. One of the most important questions to ask yourself is:

'Who is going to have to read my notes?'

1 If they are just for your own use, then there are only two rules:

- make your notes as short as possible
- make sure that you can understand them later.

2 If you are writing for someone else, then you have to think about whether they will be able to understand what you have written.
3 If you are writing notes for a particular subject teacher, then you will probably be told how the notes should be presented.

A13 *Building a story*

This unit is about storytelling. These pictures tell the beginning of a story. As you work through the unit you should make notes of your thoughts and reactions. Don't worry if all your ideas are incomplete or don't join up properly. Just focus on using your imagination as fully as you can.

Begin by writing down your ideas about:

■ the girl – what she looks like
  – what kind of person you think she is.
■ the setting – what the area is like and what kind of people live there.

- Who was the girl expecting to find there?
- What do you think has happened?
- What do you think her thoughts and feelings are?

- Who is the note from?
- Who is it to?
- What does it say?
- What are the girl's thoughts and feelings as she reads it?

- Where has the girl gone?
- Why?
- What are her thoughts and feelings at this point?
- Who does she meet?
- What do they talk about ?

What happens next?

You have been thinking about the beginning of a story and how it develops. We could be close to the end at this point, or the story could continue for quite a while.

- How many ways can you think of to continue the story?
- Jot them down briefly.
- Think about each one.
- Decide which one you like best.

The elements

You now have the makings of a complete story. Before you can write it, you need to think a little more about the elements of your story.

Character
Think about the characters, especially the central character. For each one, think about:

- their name(s)
- what they look like and how they move
- their personalities
- how they speak
- how they get on with other people.

Setting
Make sure that you really **know** the places where the story takes place. If necessary draw a little map to show how things fit together. Imagine exactly what each place is like. Think, too, about the times of day when things happen and what the weather is like.

Plot
Think carefully about:

- the order in which things happen
- how one thing leads to another.

The telling

Now tell your story.

A14 *Describing*

This is how a Year 10 student described a close friend:

My friend is a girl who is 14 years old, 5'4" and loves animals. She has one dog, 1 cat, and 2 fish. She goes out with a boy called Danny, has short, dyed, red hair, 4 earrings in one ear and 4 in the other. She sometimes wears black nail varnish and has a great personality and loves a laugh and a joke at all times. We have been friends since we were little but we are best of friends now.

Reading

1 Read the description carefully and try to create a picture of the person in your mind.
2 If you wanted to get a really clear picture of what this person looked like, what else would you want to know about her? Make a list of the questions you would want to ask.

We gave the description to three different artists. On the opposite page you can see what they produced.

3 Which do you think is the best likeness?
4 Why do you think the artists produced such different drawings from the same description?
5 What advice would you give the writer for her next attempt at writing a description?

Writing

Now choose a person you know well and write a description of them. Remember the questions you asked and the comments you made on the description above!

Some points to think about are:

- physical appearance
- clothing
- behaviour.

Remember to give as much detail as you can.

Artist 1

Artist 2

Artist 3

Describing a place

The photographs on these two pages show the Old Port at La Rochelle in western France.

1 Look at the photographs carefully. Make a list of all the details you notice which might be useful when writing a description.
2 Imagine that you are standing on the quayside. Write a list of what you can:

- see
- hear
- feel
- smell.

3 Now think carefully about the writing topic below and use your lists as the basis for a piece of descriptive writing about La Rochelle.

Lost

At the beginning of a short story, the central character is lost in this area, separated from the person(s) they were with. Describe the character's impressions, thoughts, and feelings and what they see as they wander round.

Think about how **you** would feel if you were in this foreign place and try to put those feelings into words. At first you might simply enjoy the sights and then you might gradually become more and more concerned.

1

2

Picture 2 was taken here

Picture 4 was taken here

Picture 3 was taken here

The Old Port

Lantern Tower

Picture 1 was taken here

St Nicholas Tower

4

3

Explaining

A story tells you what happened. A description tells you what something or someone is like. An **explanation** tells you:

- how to do something
- how something works, or what something or someone does.

A good writer:

- thinks about the problems people may have in understanding the explanation
- makes sure that any difficult words or ideas are explained carefully
- divides the topic up into clear sections and puts them in the best possible order
- does not go through things so quickly that people reading cannot keep up.

A shipwright is someone who does many kinds of repairs and work on boats. Below a shipwright, Adrian Wombwell, describes his work.

Read the text and look at the pictures. Write the answers to the questions after each section. You will need your answers later on.

Where he lives and works

We live by the coast in Essex. There's quite a big marina there and I work in the marina. There's also a company that installs Volvo engines and I do all the work for them, making engine covers, instrument panels – anything that they might need when they fit a new engine into a boat.

marina: a harbour for small boats

His workshop

I have a boat-building shed, a workshop; it's
48 feet by 18, with quite large doors on each
end so I can get quite big boats in.

I've got a planer-thicknesser, a bandsaw
and a circular saw and all the hand tools that
I need: routers, electric planers, sanders, disk-
cutters – plus all the traditional handtools:
adzes, drawknives, planes.

There's a lot of specialized tools that are
just used for boatbuilding. It takes a long
time to be able to use them properly.

Questions

1 Where does Adrian live?
2 Name two places where he works.
3 Name four tools he uses.

Repairs and renewals

There's all manner of repairs. People are forever
coming and saying, 'Can you fix this? I've broken
my mast ... I've broken my rudder.'

There was an instance quite recently where a
boat started leaking badly so they came into
Tollesbury. They phoned the marina and said, 'Is
there anybody that can help us?' And I said, 'Yes,'
so they brought the boat in. The boat was hauled
out and I repaired the problem. It was leaking
along the plank at the bottom. We fixed it and
they went back in the water the next day and
sailed off ...

People like to change the inside of their boat.
They might buy a new boat and there are things
that they're not happy with, they want things
altered.

Questions

4 This section describes two different
kinds of work Adrian does. What are
they?
5 Look at the photographs on these
two pages. What new ideas do they
give you about Adrian, the work he
does, and the place he works in?

The Heinemann English Programme 4 – Foundation

A new way of life

I used to sell trucks and vans which was a pretty tedious job, really. It involved charging round the countryside. With this job I can please myself. It's a satisfying thing to do, to be able to work with wood, there's not so much pressure. I don't have to travel either. I just walk a few hundred yards from my house and you meet some really interesting people.

Questions

6 What was Adrian's last job?
7 How did he feel about it?
8 He gives three reasons why he prefers his present way of life. What are they?

Preparing to write

1 You have been asked to write a short article for your school magazine, explaining:

- who Adrian is
- what he does.

It will have four paragraphs:

a who Adrian is and where he lives and works
b the repair work he does
c the other kinds of work he does
d how he feels about his work.

Make a list of all the facts you need to put in each paragraph:

Example

> (a) who Adrian is and where he lives and works
>
> **Facts:**   ● a shipwright
>   ● lives by the Essex coast

Writing

2 Now write the first draft of your article. Use your notes but don't look at the printed text in the book.
3 When you have finished, read through your writing and check it against the printed text and pictures. Have you missed out anything important? If so, write it down underneath your first draft.
4 Now read **Explaining** on page 46. Have you been 'a good writer'? Make a list of any changes you need to make.
5 Write a second draft, adding the extra information and making the changes.

A16 *What do you think?*

Argument and persuasion

It is important to be able to express your opinions clearly and convincingly. We often need to persuade other people to agree with us, or to do something we think they should. To argue or persuade effectively you need to:

- know clearly what you think
- have a set of main ideas
- have supporting arguments and/or evidence for each main idea.
- write or speak clearly and with confidence.

Outlaw this killer sport

New calls for ban after knocked-out boxer dies

These two headlines appeared in national newspapers shortly after a boxing match in which a boxer, James Murray, died after being knocked out. While he was being cared for by doctors in the ring, fighting broke out amongst the spectators, some of whom were drunk. The events led to a debate in the press and on radio and television about whether boxing should be banned.

Your opinion now

Before you start looking at the arguments, what is your opinion about this subject?

> Should boxing be banned or not? Or are you a 'Don't know'?

The arguments

On pages 50 and 51 the opposing arguments are presented. Look at both pages carefully and then turn to the instructions on page 52.

For a ban

Main ideas	Supporting arguments/evidence
Boxing is the only sport in which contestants have deliberately to hurt each other in order to win.	■ in other sports violence against your opponent is penalised ■ in boxing you win by hitting your opponent more than he hits you – or by knocking him out
Boxing matches are organised so that they encourage violence.	■ newspapers and TV reports focus on knockouts, strength of punch, and heavyweight boxers
The rules make the boxer's head the main target for his opponent.	■ you score points for hitting it ■ it makes a knockout possible
This leads to brain damage or death.	■ many boxers suffer brain damage because the effects build up over time ■ some are killed or severely damaged in just one bout
A sport that leads directly to severe brain damage or death is not acceptable in a civilised society.	■ many of our laws are passed to **stop** people attacking and hurting each other. Boxers are encouraged to do just that

Against a ban

Main ideas	Supporting arguments/evidence
Boxing is part of our national sporting life.	■ it has always offered tough young men a route out of poverty and into a better life ■ it has produced popular heroes like Henry Cooper
Many sports are dangerous.	■ just as many people die in motor racing and football ■ mountaineering is even more dangerous ■ people will always seek the thrill of danger
If you introduced a ban, boxing would still go on – illegally.	■ it is impossible to ban something that is so popular ■ while it is legal you can control it and make it safer – if it goes on illegally you cannot do that
Instead of banning it, we should make it safer.	■ there is already good medical support both before and during bouts – this should be strengthened ■ championship bouts should be reduced in length – most of the injuries happen towards the end of long bouts ■ boxers should wear heavier gloves so that it is more difficult for them to harm each other ■ there should be better crowd control and alcohol should be banned

Talking points

- Have you changed your opinion at all after looking at the arguments?
- Which case has the stronger argument and why?
- Are there any points you think should be added to either argument?

Decision time

Decide where you stand on this issue:

A **for a ban**
B **against a ban**
C **on the fence** – you can see the arguments on both sides.

Make a plan

Make a list of all the points you need to make in support of your opinion:

- choose from the material on pages 50 and 51
- add any ideas of your own
- if you are arguing for or against, make sure that you can knock down the opposing ideas.

Look at what you have written and sort your ideas into a good order.
In particular:

- make sure that each idea follows on from the previous one
- introduce your writing by explaining briefly what the subject is
- finish with a good strong expression of your opinion.

Draft

Now you are going to write an article for a teenage magazine, expressing your point of view. Write your first draft. Some important points to remember:

1 Think carefully about how to begin. Your **introduction** should give the reader an idea of where you stand.
2 In the main part of the article, make sure that you have backed up what you say with **reasons and evidence**.
3 Your article should have a **conclusion** in which you sum up what you have said. Try to leave the reader with something to think about.

When you have finished, read it through to make sure it says exactly what you think. If possible get someone else to read it and comment on it.

Final version

Write your final version and include any changes you have decided on.

 There is an exam practice paper and mark scheme for this unit in the Teacher's File

A17 *Dear Sir or Madam ...*

Writing letters to people you do not know

One of the most difficult writing situations is when you have to write a letter to a person whom you have never met. There are three things to think about.

Content
Your letter needs to be planned so that it explains things clearly and in the right order.

Form
Your letter should be set out correctly.

Tone
You should use a suitable tone in the words and sentences you use.

Content

This kind of letter must contain these three parts.

Introduction
A short paragraph in which you explain to the reader what the letter is about. This saves a lot of time; if you are writing to a company, for example, it means that they can pass the letter to the right person.

Body of the letter
One or more paragraphs in which you explain clearly what you have to say.

Conclusion
A short paragraph which 'winds up' the letter. It should spell out to the reader what the purpose of your letter is. (For example, if you want them to **do** something, it should make this clear.)

The sample letter on page 54 contains each of these three parts. It also has an explanation of the form and tone of this type of letter.

Setting out a formal letter

19 Redmond Drive

Hattershall

West Midlands

B98 5TF

Your address
Look at how it
is lined up

Mr E. Sinclair

Customer Services Department

Future CDRoms

Greystoke Industrial Estate

Crewe

CR32 6BC

*The name and
address of the
person you are
writing to*

23rd March 1996

The date (in full)

Dear Mr Sinclair

The greeting
There is more about
this in **Tone**

'Future Multimedia Encyclopaedia'

Heading
You don't have to
put this, but it helps
to make it clear
what the letter is
about

I recently returned to you a faulty copy of this CD-ROM. You promised
to send me a replacement 'by return'.

Introduction

The replacement copy did not arrive until three weeks later. When we
put it in the machine we discovered that it was not the 'Future
Multimedia Encyclopaedia' at all, but a collection of games for 9-year-
olds. We bought the original faulty copy at the beginning of January. It
is now the end of March and we still have not got the goods we paid
for.

Body of the letter

I shall be grateful if you will return the purchase price of £29.99.
Your CD-ROM is enclosed.

Conclusion

Yours sincerely

Ending
There is more about
this in **Tone**

G.F. Harrison

Tone

Greeting

If you know the name of the person you are writing to, then it is a good idea to use it in the greeting. The correct form is *Dear* plus the title, normally *Mr*, *Mrs*, *Miss* or *Ms*. If you are writing to a woman and do not know the title she prefers, it is best to use *Ms*. This offends very few people, while using *Mrs* or *Miss* in the wrong situation can be very irritating.

If you do not know the name of the person you are writing to, then you will have to use the form *Dear Sir or Madam*.

Ending

If you have used the name of the person you are writing to, you end with *Yours sincerely*, followed by your signature, giving your initials and last name. If you have started *Dear Sir or Madam*, then you should end *Yours faithfully*, followed by the same signature.

Style

Remember that you are writing to someone you have never met and want to make the correct impression on them. Normally you should follow these rules:

1 Do not use slang or dialect words and phrases.
2 Do not use short forms like *haven't* or *I'll*.
3 Do not write in a very personal way. (For example, in the letter opposite it would not be suitable to use expressions like, 'I was ever so upset.')

A trip to the US of A

Read this advertisement and then write a letter applying for an exchange. Remember to write:

1 An introduction
Explain to Mr. Bryan what you are writing about.
2 The body of the letter
This could have two paragraphs:
- one covering points 1, 2 and 3 in the advertisement
- one covering point 4 in the advertisement.
3 The conclusion
This should cover point 5 in the advertisement.

Take a break in the States!

Under the new UK/US student exchange deal, students aged 15–20 can now spend up to two months in the USA on an all-expenses-paid exchange.

How it works

You write a letter to *UK-US Exchange*. Tell us about yourself:
1 where you live and study
2 your interests and leisure activities
3 what you are studying at school
4 why you would like to go the States
5 why you would be a good person to represent your country abroad.

We will choose the twenty best letters and match them to the twenty best US students. The winners will then exchange homes and lives for 6–9 weeks this summer.

Interested?

Write to Al J. Bryan Jr, UK-US Exchange, PO Box 000, London. W1X 99M.

5

10

15

A18 *Writing a newspaper report*

Researching the story

When journalists write reports they usually try to answer these questions:

Who was involved?
What happened?
When?
Where?
Why did it happen?

Organising the story

People often do not have time to read the whole of a newspaper story, so stories are usually written in this order:

1 Main story
2 Interesting details
3 Background information and comments.

The parts of a newspaper report

Headline
This should be striking or amusing in order to catch the reader's eye.

Byline
This tells us who wrote the report.

Lead paragraph
This should be short. It introduces the story, holds our attention, and makes us want to read more.

Main story
The whole story is told briefly and simply, so that a reader who just wants to know what happened can grasp it quickly and easily.

Interesting details

Background information
For people who want to know a little more about the story.

Comments
By people who were involved.

Hamster gets his ticket to ride

By PHILIP DERBYSHIRE

SWEEP the hamster got his very own bus pass yesterday.

Embarrassed officials from West Midlands Travel made the gesture after 11-year-old Wayne Bass was made to buy a 45p ticket for the school pet by an over-zealous bus driver.

At a presentation at Lode Heath School, Solihull, Wayne was given a £47.90 scholar's bus pass, valid for next term.

And Sweep received a pass worth £4.70.

Wayne, of Sheldon, Birmingham, had taken Sweep home for the weekend. But when he boarded the bus to Solihull on Monday morning he was

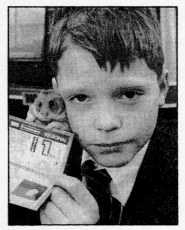

FREE TRIPS: Sweep and Wayne

made to pay for the hamster on top of his own 36p fare.

Mr Phil Bakeman, spokesman for West Midlands Travel, Britain's biggest bus company, apologised and said the driver may have been suffering from Monday morning blues.

He said: "We definitely owe Wayne and his parents an apology and this is our way of trying to put things right."

He added it was not company policy to issue animals with passes and as far as he knew this was a first in Britain.

After the hour-long presentation in a single-decker bus, Wayne said: "I am happy with the way the company have sorted it out. I was put off travelling by bus, but I've got a pass now so I can't complain and will still use the bus."

Paul Ashton, general manager at Lea Hall bus station, said he would be interviewing the offending driver.

He said: "I'll be giving him a little pet-talk and if needs be we can take disciplinary action.

"He's taken a lot of ribbing from his mates over this."

Cult

Wayne's headmaster, Graham Robb, said Sweep had become a cult figure in the school and even had his own timetable made up for him.

"The children here also keep some stick insects and another hamster, and I'm seeing if we can get a pass for them too," he said.

"West Midlands Travel recognise that they were wrong and they have now put it right.

"I'm glad we can now see the funny side of it."

The Heinemann English Programme 4 – Foundation

Problem child

You are a reporter on a local paper and this is a page from your notebook. You have been given the information over the phone by a colleague. Now you are going to follow up the story. Read the notes and then follow the instructions below.

- allegations that an eight-year-old boy attacks other children:
  - attacks pensioners
  - throws stones at windows
  - rips up plants/bushes/trees
- allegations that nine-year-old sister is also involved
- complaints from fourteen neighbours in West Bromwich
- have contacted police
- response: 'We are taking the complaints seriously'
- age of children means that the police cannot take action
- have contacted social services
- social services met yesterday: possibility of taking into care
- have contacted local MP Michael Forton
- children cannot be named for legal reasons

A Researching the story

1 Do you know enough to write the story? If not, what questions would you still like to ask? Write them down.
2 Make up answers to your questions, but make sure they fit in with the information you already have.

B Organising the story

3 Make a brief plan for your report. (Look at **The parts of a newspaper report** on page 56.) Give each paragraph a number and a title that describes what it will contain.

C Writing the story

4 Now write a first draft of the story.
5 When you have written it, think of a suitable headline.

Work with a partner.
6 Swap with your partner. Read and comment on each other's work.
7 Write a final draft, taking note of the comments that your partner made.

A19 *Writing an article*

Articles

Magazines contain a number of different things, from stories to advertising, but an important part of all magazines is their **articles**.

A magazine article is a piece of writing, usually between 400 and 1500 words long, about a clearly defined subject. Articles:

- give information
- communicate ideas
- put across a point of view
- provide entertainment.

Before you start

Before starting to write an article, you need to be very sure about three things:

Subject
- Are you clear exactly what you want to write about?
- Have you got all the information you need, or do you need to do some research?

Purpose
- What is your purpose in writing? (For example: to entertain? to inform? to persuade? a mixture of these?)

Audience
- Exactly who are you writing for? Think about your readers':

  - age
  - sex
  - interests
  - background knowledge of the subject.

Anatomy of an article

'My baby left me terrified'

Like many people, Penny Hersey, 31, from Selmeston, East Sussex, had never liked heights.
5 *But her fear developed into a full phobia after the birth of her first child …*

When my daughter Hayley was born nine 10 years ago, I found the whole experience really stressful. I'd always been slightly nervous of heights, but, for some reason, it started to 15 get worse.

Now I know that, as the stress of looking after the baby increased, so did my fear of heights. By the time 20 my third child was born, I couldn't go anywhere that wasn't at ground level.

Shopping arcades were a nightmare with all their 25 different levels. Even the cinema was a problem unless I sat in the stalls.

When my marriage broke up, I started to panic just thinking about heights. But 30 my worst moment was when I married my new husband Ken and he took me on honeymoon to Paris.

When we arrived at the 35 airport I discovered that the only way to the arrivals lounge was up a steep, glass-encased escalator. I was terrified. Ken had to hide my 40 head in his coat so I couldn't see. I felt sick and shaky for the next three days and it ruined my honeymoon.

I finally got help last year 45 when I attended a course to help people suffering from phobias.

It taught me how to look at the painful, stressful areas 50 of my life in an objective way. Once I saw where my phobia had come from, I was able to overcome it.

Now at last I can live again 55 – I can even go to Brighton, walk on the pier and look down at the waves.

Your article

Now it is your turn. You are going to write a short article on phobias for a magazine of your choice. Look again at **Before you start** on page 59 which gives some general advice about how to approach this.

1 Look carefully at the materials in Phobias. Make sure you understand it all.
2 Decide on the type of magazine you are writing for.
3 Think about your approach. (Look at the suggestions in the box **Who and Why?**) Now make a plan.
4 Write your article.

Who and Why?

You can think of your own magazine and audience, or you can choose from these:

Audience
- teenagers
- children at primary school
- retired people.

Purpose
- to inform
- to reassure
- to entertain.

Phobias

Life in the modern world has always been stressful. But in the past few years, things have got worse. We've had to cope with recession, repossession of property, redundancy, a soaring divorce rate, too much work, or even no work, and the choice between career and parenthood ... or both.

And the more stress we suffer, the more we risk becoming ruled by an irrational terror – a phobia.

FACT: One in 4 people suffers from a phobia – that's 14 million people in Britain.

FACT: One in 10 phobics' lives is ruined because of their fear.

FACT: Calls for help to just one of the phobic support groups have increased by 500 per cent in the past three years.

Woman's Own

10 MOST COMMON PHOBIAS

AGORAPHOBIA	fear of open or public spaces
SOCIAL PHOBIA	fear of being watched in public
CLAUSTROPHOBIA	fear of enclosed spaces
ARACHNOPHOBIA	fear of spiders
AEROPHOBIA	fear of air travel
ACROPHOBIA	fear of heights
ODONTOPHOBIA	fear of going to the dentist
NOSOPHOBIA	fear of disease
ORNITHOPHOBIA	fear of birds
TRYPANOPHOBIA	fear of injections

A20 *What were they like?*

Character

We can learn about characters in novels and plays from:

1 what the storyteller tells us about them
2 what they say
3 what they do
4 what other characters say about them.

Read these short extracts. Then look at the instructions at the top of the next page.

The visitor

He was small and plump, with a plump face that had a greyness about it where he shaved; his hair was grey also, falling to a fringe on his forehead. He was untidily
5 dressed, a turtle-necked red jersey beneath a jacket that had a ballpoint pen and a pencil sticking out of the breast pocket. When he stood up his black corduroy trousers developed concertina creases.

William Trevor: *Lovers of their time*

Lucy

'Where does the sun go when it's night-time?' she demanded, aged about four.
'It goes to bed,' replied
5 Maureen comfortably. 'It goes bye-byes, just like you do. All tucked up. And then it wakes up in the morning and shines in at your window, doesn't it?'
10 Lucy heard her in silence, her mouth knotted in disapproval. And then she burst out, 'No, it doesn't. It can't because it's not a girl.'

Penelope Lively: *Cleopatra's sister*

Boddser Brown

Chas hated Boddser; he had round spectacles and cropped hair like a German, and a great gangling grown-up body. He was stupid and a bully; an arm-twister who made his pleasure last a long time. One day last term he and his gang held a kid's head down the toilet and flushed it three times. The kid
5 nearly drowned and was off school for a week. Boddser got caned, but you might as well cane a rhinoceros. Chas sometimes dreamt of beating in his skull with an iron bar.

But he could never leave Boddser alone; he was so easy to take the mickey out of ... Boddser was nearly as afraid of laughter as Chas was of Boddser's
10 fists. Taking the mickey out of Boddser was like bullfighting; deadly but fun.

Robert Westall: *The Machine-gunners*

Appearances

1 Which of these three illustrations looks most like your impression of **The visitor**?

2 What are your reasons?

3 Which of these three illustrations looks most like your impression of **Boddser Brown**?

4 What are your reasons?

5 In the extract called 'Lucy' what do you think **Maureen** looks like and why?

What is the evidence?

At the top of page 62 are listed four different ways in which we learn about characters. How did you learn about each of these three characters?

Writing a character study

When we write about characters, we can describe:

1 **Appearance:** what they look like
2 **Behaviour:** how they behave and what it tells us about them
3 **Personality:** what they are like as people.

In each case we must back up what we say by referring to one of the points in the **Character** list on page 62.

Boddser Brown

Appearance ▶ He was very large for his age and physically strong, but awkward; he had 'a great gangling grown-up body'.

Behaviour ▶ He was a bully and had formed a gang which terrorised younger and smaller children at school. For example they nearly killed one child by holding his 'head down the toilet and flushing it three times'.

Personality ▶ Like many bullies he has weak points of which he is afraid. He hates being made fun of and laughed at.

You try

1 Read the description of **The visitor**. Think about what we learn about his **appearance** from the text. Write a description of what he looks like, using your own words.
2 Look at what you have written and think about this man. What do you imagine he is like as a person? Write what you think and why you think it.
3 Read the description of **Lucy** and **Maureen**. Write what we learn about their **personalities** from the text.

TF You will find further practice for this unit using texts from other cultures and traditions in the Teacher's File.

Big Foot

Read this character description and then follow
the instructions at the bottom of the page.

> Big Foot was really big and really black, and everybody in Miguel Street was
> afraid of him. It wasn't his bigness or his blackness that people feared, for
> there were blacker and bigger people about. People were afraid of him
> because he was so silent and sulky; he *looked* dangerous, like those terrible
> 5 dogs that never bark but just look at you from the corner of their eyes.
>
> Hat used to say, 'Is only a form of showing off, you know all this quietness
> he does give us. He quiet just because he ain't have anything to say, that's all.'
>
> Yet you could hear Hat telling all sorts of people at the races and cricket,
> 'Big Foot and me? We is bosom pals, man. We grow up together.'
>
> 10 And at school I myself used to say, 'Big Foot does live in my street, you
> hear. I know him good good, and if any one of all you touch me, I go tell Big
> Foot.'
>
> At that time I had never spoken a single word to Big Foot.
>
> We in Miguel Street were proud to claim him because he was something of
> 15 a character in Port of Spain, and had quite a reputation. It was Big Foot who
> flung the stone at Radio Trinidad building one day and broke a window. When
> the magistrate asked why he did it, Big Foot just said, 'To wake them up.'
>
> A well-wisher paid the fine for him. Then there was the time he got a job
> driving one of the diesel-buses. He drove the bus out of the city to Carenage,
> 20 five miles away, and told the passengers to get out and bathe. He stood by to
> see that they did.
>
> After that he got a job as a postman, and he had a great time misplacing
> people's letters. They found him at Dock site, with the bag half full of letters,
> soaking his big feet in the Gulf of Paria.
>
> 25 He said, 'Is hard work, walking all over the place, delivering people letters.
> You come like a postage stamp, man.'
>
> All Trinidad thought of him as a comedian but we who knew him thought
> otherwise.

V.S. Naipaul: *Miguel Street*

What to do

1 Read the text again carefully, making notes
on all the **information** you can find about:

- what he looks like
- how he behaves
- what his personality is like.

2 Make sure that you can support each of the
things you have found with some **evidence**
from the text.

3 Use your notes to write a character study
of Big Foot.

This extract comes from the beginning of a short story. As you reach the end of each section, answer the questions beside it **before** going on to the next section.

The gentle assassin

By noon, when Dr Jamieson arrived in London, all entrances into the city had been sealed since six o'clock that morning. The Coronation Day crowds had waited in their places along the procession route for almost
5 twenty-four hours, and Green Park was deserted as Dr Jamieson slowly made his way up the sloping grass toward the Underground station below the Ritz. Abandoned haversacks and sleeping bags lay about among the litter under the trees, and twice Dr Jamieson
10 stumbled slightly. By the time he reached the Station entrance he was perspiring freely, and sat down on a bench, resting his heavy gun-metal suitcase on the grass.

Questions

1 What does the title suggest the story is going to be about?
2 Is there anything in this first section to back this up?
3 What does Dr Jamieson do in this section? Is there anything out of the ordinary in his behaviour?

Directly in front of him was one of the high wooden
stands. He could see the backs of the top row of
15   spectators, women in bright summer dresses, men in
shirtsleeves, newspapers shielding their heads from the
hot sunlight, parties of children singing and waving their
Union Jacks. All the way down Piccadilly the office
blocks were crammed with people leaning out of
20   windows, and the street was a mass of colour and noise.
Now and then bands played in the distance, or an officer
in charge of the troops lining the route bellowed an
order and re-formed his men.
      Dr Jamieson listened with interest to all these sounds,
25   savouring the sun-filled excitement.

In his middle sixties, he was a small neat figure with
greying hair and alert sensitive eyes. His forehead was
broad, with a marked slope, which made his somewhat
professorial manner appear more youthful. This was
30   helped by the rakish cut of his grey silk suit, its ultra-
narrow lapels fastened by a single embroidered button,
heavy braided seams on the sleeves and trousers. As
someone emerged from the first-aid marquee at the far
end of the stand and walked toward him Dr Jamieson
35   sensed the discrepancy between their attire – the man
was wearing a baggy blue suit with huge flapping lapels –
and frowned to himself in annoyance. Glancing at his
watch, he picked up the suitcase and hurried into the
Underground station.

J.G. Ballard: *The day of forever*

rakish: *jaunty*
marquee: *large tent*
discrepancy: *strong contrast*

Questions

4 What does Dr Jamieson do
in this section?
5 What do you think is the
purpose of this part of the
story?

Questions

6 What actions take place in this
section?
7 What do we learn about
Dr Jamieson's thoughts and
feelings?
8 What does this section add
to our understanding of
Dr Jamieson and what he
is doing?

What next?

1 Think again about the title. What did it lead you to
think the story would be about?
2 Have the opening paragraphs added to your ideas
about how the story will develop?
3 What do you think is going to happen and why?

Action

Stories describe action. Writers do this in different ways:

- by telling us directly what happens
- by hinting and leaving us to work things out for ourselves
- through conversation.

We need action in a story to keep it moving along. Action also has other purposes:

- it tells us about characters. We learn a lot from the way people behave
- to maintain tension, so that we want to go on reading.

The killer

This extract comes from the beginning of a novel. Read it and then answer the questions at the end.

Murder didn't mean much to Raven. It was just a new job. You had to be careful. You had to use your brains. It was not a question of hatred. He had only seen the Minister once: he had been pointed out to Raven as he walked down the new housing estate between the
5 small, lit Christmas trees, an old, grubby man without friends, who was said to love humanity.

The cold wind cut Raven's face in the wide Continental street. It was a good excuse for turning the collar of his coat well above his mouth. A hare-lip was a serious handicap in his profession; it had
10 been badly sewn in infancy, so that now the upper lip was twisted and scarred. When you carried about so easy an identification you couldn't help becoming ruthless in your methods. It had always, from the first, been necessary for Raven to eliminate a witness.

He carried an attaché case. He looked like any other youngish
15 man going home after his work; his dark overcoat had a clerical air. He moved steadily up the street like hundreds of his kind. A tram went by, lit up in the early dusk: he didn't take it. An economical young man, you might have thought, saving money for his home. Perhaps even now he was on his way to meet his girl.
20 But Raven had never had a girl. The hare-lip prevented that. He had learnt, when he was very young, how repulsive it was. He turned into one of the tall grey houses and climbed the stairs, a sour bitter screwed-up figure.

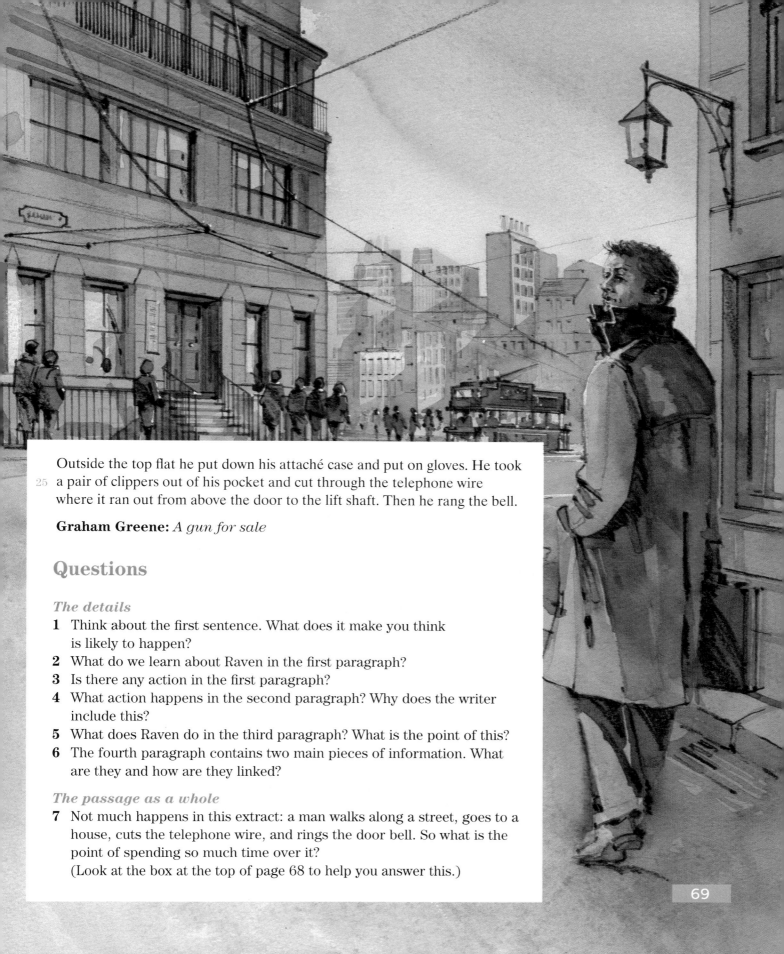

Outside the top flat he put down his attaché case and put on gloves. He took
25 a pair of clippers out of his pocket and cut through the telephone wire
where it ran out from above the door to the lift shaft. Then he rang the bell.

Graham Greene: *A gun for sale*

Questions

The details
1 Think about the first sentence. What does it make you think
   is likely to happen?
2 What do we learn about Raven in the first paragraph?
3 Is there any action in the first paragraph?
4 What action happens in the second paragraph? Why does the writer
   include this?
5 What does Raven do in the third paragraph? What is the point of this?
6 The fourth paragraph contains two main pieces of information. What
   are they and how are they linked?

The passage as a whole
7 Not much happens in this extract: a man walks along a street, goes to a
   house, cuts the telephone wire, and rings the door bell. So what is the
   point of spending so much time over it?
   (Look at the box at the top of page 68 to help you answer this.)

Viewpoint

The same story can be told in many different ways. In particular the writer has to decide from which point of view he will tell the story. For example:

First person

This is sometimes called an 'I' story. The writer 'pretends' to be the central character and tells the story as if they were that person.

Third person

The writer stands 'outside' the story and describes it as if they were watching what is going on. This can be done in different ways:

1

We see the events of the story through the eyes of one or more of the characters and the writer helps us to imagine very fully what is going on in that character's mind.

2

The writer stands back from the events of the story and describes them as if they were like a god, looking down from above.

As you read these three extracts, decide the answers to these questions:

- Does the author take us inside a character's thoughts and feelings?
- Is it first person or third person storytelling?

A

Comfort Jones was running. She had never run as fast as this or as far, she hadn't known she could. Right across Kensington Gardens and up the Broad Walk with the carrier bag of shopping banging against her legs and her breath scraping in her throat as if she had swallowed barbed wire. She passed Kensington Palace but she didn't see
5 the slivers of brown brick and white paint between the green trees. She didn't even see the Round Pond on the other side like a mirror dropped in the grass. She ran right through a flock of pigeons feeding on the path.

    'Take care now, take care,' the old lady said sharply, throwing out handfuls of white bread. She had bought a whole loaf as a Saturday treat. 'Children nowadays, not a
10 scrap of manners.'

    But Comfort didn't hear the old lady, only the slap of her own sandals on the asphalt path and the flutter of wings in her face as the pigeons rose in a grey cloud around her.

Geraldine Kaye: *Comfort herself*

B

Anyone who has never before visited Krishnapur, and who approaches from the east, is likely to think he has reached the end of his journey a few miles sooner than he expected. While still some distance from Krishnapur he begins to ascend a shallow ridge. From here he will see what appears to be a town in the heat distorted distance. He will see the white glitter of walls and roofs and a handsome grove of trees, perhaps even the dome of what might be a temple. Round about there will be the unending plain still, exactly as it has been for many miles back, a dreary ocean of bald earth, in the immensity of which an occasional field of sugar cane or mustard is utterly lost.

The surprising thing is that this plain is not quite deserted, as one might expect. As he crosses it towards the white walls in the distance the traveller may notice an occasional figure way out somewhere between the road and the horizon, a man walking with a burden on his head in one direction or another ...

J.G. Farrell: *The siege of Krishnapur*

C

On Monday morning Mum took me to the doctor's. The waiting room was covered with posters saying 'Don't let your baby nudge you into going to the doctor's.' I'd never noticed them before. I felt ashamed.

It wasn't my usual doctor. His examination was quick and professional. He told Mum I was probably twelve weeks' pregnant. My stomach plunged, even though I had known it for ages, for ever, it seemed. Everything felt as if it was draining out of me. To hear it said so clinically and finally was like being told 'Tomorrow you will hang' or something. I remember saying, 'I don't want a baby,' in a tiny weak voice that didn't sound like mine, and Mum sat there with her lips pursed tight while the doctor told us that if a termination was to take place it must be before sixteen weeks. 'Otherwise it will be very traumatic for you,' he said. My tears were as sharp as needles. I couldn't take in what he was saying. I have a baby inside me.

Berlie Doherty: *Dear Nobody*

Three generations ...

This extract comes from the opening chapter of a novel. Read it and as you do so, think carefully about whose point of view you are seeing things from.

Three months ago, his grandmother died, and then they had moved to this house.
'I will not live there again, until it belongs to me,' his father had said, though the old man lay upstairs, after a second stroke, and lingered, giving no trouble.
The boy was taken up to see him. 'You must not be afraid,' his father said,
5   nervously, 'he is a very old man, now, very ill.'

'I am never afraid.' And that was no more than the truth, though his father would not have believed it.
It will be very moving, Joseph Hooper had decided, with the three generations together and one upon his death bed, the eldest son of the eldest son of the eldest
10   son. For, in middle age, he was acquiring a dynastic sense.

a dynastic sense: a feeling of being part of a family that went back a long way

But it had not been moving. The old man had breathed noisily, and dribbled a little, and never woken. The sick room smelled sour.

'Ah, well,' Mr Hooper had said and coughed, 'he is very ill, you know. But I am glad you have seen him.'

'Why?'

'Well – because you are his only grandson. His heir, I suppose. Yes. It is only as it should be.'

The boy looked towards the bed. His skin is already dead, he thought, it is old and dry. But he saw that the bones of the eye-sockets, and the nose and jaw, showed through it and gleamed. Everything about him, from the stubble of hair down to the folded line of sheet, was bleached and grey-ish white.

'All he looks like,' Edmund Hooper said, 'is one of his dead old moths.'

'That is not the way to speak! You must show respect.'

His father had led him out. Though *I* am only able to show respect now, he thought, to behave towards my father as I should, because he is dying, he is almost gone away from me.

Edmund Hooper, walking down the great staircase into the wood-panelled hall, thought nothing of his grandfather. But later, he remembered the moth-like whiteness of the very old skin.

Susan Hill: *I'm the king of the castle*

Thinking about the viewpoint

This story is told in the **third person**. It is not as straightforward as the examples you have looked at so far. These questions will help you to work out what is going on.

1 How many characters are there in this extract? Who are they?
2 Look again at lines 1–3. Do they take us inside the thoughts and feelings of any of the characters?
3 Lines 4–17 describe events mainly from the point of view of one of the characters:

   ■ who is it?
   ■ what do we learn about his thoughts and feelings in these lines?

4 In line 18 the viewpoint changes. How can you tell?
5 Does the viewpoint stay with this character until the end of the extract?

Writing

Part of this story shows us the thoughts and feelings of Edmund Hooper about his sick grandfather. Imagine that you are him and you later tell a friend at school what happened. Write your version of the events.

A23 *What you think ...*

Conversation in literature

When you have a conversation with someone, the words you say often reflect the thoughts that are going on inside your head – or some of them. In stories and plays, writers can suggest to us what people are thinking by what they say.

If we are going to understand the thoughts of the characters, we often have to do quite a lot of detective work. Sometimes a writer gives us a bit more help. The picture story that follows is based on a play by Alan Ayckbourn.

'Where's she gone? Making the tea. I haven't heard the whistle. I'll have to get up and carry the tray in when I hear the whistle. I don't know why I ever offered to start carrying the thing in the first place.'

'I've been carrying trays in and out of the door ever since. If they were heavy I'd understand it. I do nothing except walk from here to the kitchen, from the kitchen to here with that tray. It's empty most of the time anyway. Still I suppose it's a nice gesture. At least I do it every day. Not just when we have visitors.

That tea must be ready by now. Haven't heard the whistle. If she's left the whistle off the kettle it'll be the first time ... And she talks about me leaving the whistle off.'

'What's happened to him this evening? Must be a world crisis if he's actually forgotten to come padding out to carry this tray. Perhaps he's finally given it up. Thank heavens for that. Forever running in and out with this tray. I'd like to know what he's done with the whistle off that kettle. Where is he then?'

... and what you say

Thinking it through

- What are your first impressions of this couple?
- How long do you think they have been married?
- What are their feelings for each other?

Thinking

1. How should the words they say be spoken?
2. What should go in the empty balloons?
3. How might the conversation continue?

Improvising

Work with a partner.

4. Decide who should play the parts of Husband and Wife.
5. Act the scene shown on this page.
6. Improvise the rest of the conversation.

What happens next?

As you have seen, most of the play is the characters' thoughts spoken aloud. If the next part of the play is shown without the thoughts, so that what is left is just the actions and the words spoken aloud, you get this:

(HUSBAND *starts to stir his tea.*)

2   WIFE: It's not sugared.

     HUSBAND: Oh no? (*Laughing loudly.*) Hey! Do you know what's in the

4   sugar basin ... the whistle, the whistle off the kettle!

     WIFE: (*Laughing*) Oh really? Fancy. How silly of me.

6   HUSBAND: Silly you!

(*They both laugh gaily at some length.*)

8   Oh dear.

     WIFE: Oh dear.

10 (*The* HUSBAND *laughs at something he's reading. He laughs again.*

The WIFE *laughs suddenly.*

12 *The* HUSBAND *folds the newspaper.*)

     HUSBAND: How's the boiler been today?

14   WIFE: No trouble at all today.

     HUSBAND: Good, must have learnt to behave itself at last, eh?

16 (*He chuckles.*

She laughs.)

18   You see, if you keep the air vent unclogged, you're all right.

     WIFE: So it said in the instructions.

Alan Ayckbourn: *Countdown*

Filling in the gaps

These questions will help you work out the missing thoughts.
The numbers refer to the line numbers printed in the script.

Line	Question
2	How long does the wife let the husband go on stirring his tea before telling him there's no sugar in it?
1	What is she thinking while he does so?
3	What are his thoughts when she does tell him?
5	What does each think when the whistle from the kettle is found?
6	He's blaming the wife. How does she feel about it?
7	Now he's rubbing it in. How does she feel? How does he feel?
10	What's he laughing at? How does the wife react?
11	Why does she laugh now?
12	Why does he stop reading? What does she think he's going to do?
13	He says 'today' – has there been some trouble with the boiler? Or does he always ask her the same questions? How does she feel when he asks it?
16	What is he thinking as he laughs?
17	What is she thinking as she laughs?
18	Has he told her this before? If so how does she feel?
19	What does this tell us about her? How do you think she says the line?

Your own reading

Writers don't always give us as much help as that. Often we have to work out what characters are thinking by listening to what they say. Read the following short extract and then follow the instructions at the end.

Dave Robicheaux, an ex-policeman in Louisiana has rescued a young girl from the wreck of a plane in the sea. He wants to protect her from the authorities by hiding the truth. He and his companion Annie take her to a local Catholic hospital because she has swallowed a lot of water.

We went inside, and Annie carried the little girl back to the emergency room while I sat across the reception desk from a heavyset nun in a white habit who filled out the girl's admission form.

The nun's face was as big and round as a pie plate, and her wimple was crimped as tightly across her forehead as a medieval knight's visor.

'What is her name?' she said.

I looked back at her.

'Do you know her name?' she said.

'Alafair.'

'What is her last name?'

'Robicheaux.'

'Is she your daughter?'

'Sure.'

'She's your daughter?'

'Of course.'

'Hmmm,' she said, and continued to write on the form. ⊚

Then, 'I'll look in on her for you. In the meantime, why don't you look over this information and make sure I wrote it down accurately.'

'I trust you, sister.'

'Oh, I wouldn't say that too quickly.' ⊚

She walked heavily down the hall with her black beads swinging from her waist. She had the physique of an over-the-hill prizefighter. A few minutes later she was back and I was growing more uncomfortable.

'My, what an interesting family you have,' she said. 'Did you know that your daughter speaks nothing but Spanish?' ⊚

James Lee Burke: *Heaven's prisoners*

What to do

At each point where you see this symbol, ⊚
write down what you think the nun is thinking.

A24 The moon's a balloon ... or is it?

It's a real challenge to describe things in words. Usually people have a good idea about what you are describing because they have seen something like it. Imagine what it would be like to describe everyday things like the moon to someone who had been blind from birth. When we are trying to describe a special scene or event, we often end up saying that it is like something else. For example,

The concert was brilliant: it was like the Cup Final and a massive party all rolled into one!

Creative writers do the same thing. They want to communicate their experience so they use comparisons to get across their meaning. When we study literature we look at how they do it. We also have the chance to decide how well we think they do it.

What's a moon?
Well, it's round and white.
Like a mint?
Not really.
Like a football?
Not exactly. It's more like a football than a mint.
Can you kick it?
No, stupid, it's in the sky, like a star.
What's a star?

Brainstorming

So just what is the moon like?
Find as many comparisons as you can.

1 Write down your comparisons very
   briefly.

   – The moon's a soft mint
   – a new white football

   Do not worry about the quality, just
   let your imagination take over. When
   you have run out of ideas, look back
   over them.
2 Try to rank them in order starting
   with the best and moving downwards.
3 Why do you think some are better
   than others?

Language for literature

There are several important words that help when people are discussing this kind of language.

- An **image** is a picture created by the words that a writer uses.
  Similes and metaphors are two ways in which images are created.
- A **simile** is a type of image in which one thing is said to be similar to, or **like** another.
  For example,

  Television is just like a drug to you.

  Whilst the word **like** is most often found in a simile, the word **as** is also used. For example,

  *Television is **as** mind-numbing **as** a drug.*

- A **metaphor** is another type of image. Instead of saying that something is like something
  else, it is described as if it were *actually* that thing. For example,

  He sat in the armchair getting his fix of football highlights.

  In this example, television is described as if it were literally a drug.

Summary

The moon **is like a** balloon = simile
The moon **is a** balloon = metaphor

The Heinemann English Programme 4 – Foundation

Above the dock

Above the quiet dock in midnight,
Tangled in the tall mast's corded height,
Hangs the moon. What seemed so far away
Is but a child's balloon, forgotten after play.

T. E. Hulme

Moonlight

The Moon, that peeped as she came up,
Is clear on top, with all her light;
She rests her chin on Nailsworth Hill,
And, where she looks, the World is white.

5 White with her light – or is it Frost,
Or is it Snow her eyes have seen;
Or is it Cherry blossom there,
Where no such trees have ever been?

W. H. Davies

Like a dying lady

And, like a dying lady lean and pale,
Who totters forth, wrapp'd in a gauzy veil,   **gauzy:** thin
Out of her chamber, led by the insane   **chamber:** bedroom
And feeble wanderings of her fading brain,   **insane:** mad
5 The moon arose up in the murky east   **murky:** cloudy
A white and shapeless mass.

P. B. Shelley

Questions

1 Look at the three poems and choose one simile about the moon.
Your answer could look like this:

In the poem by ...., the moon is described as being like ....

2 Look at the three poems and choose one metaphor about the moon.
Your answer could look like this:

In the poem by ...., the moon is described as if it is ....

3 Describe the scene in *Moonlight* in your own words.
4 Describe the lady in the poem *Like a dying lady.*
5 Two of the three poems describe the moon as female. Why do you think
the writers think of the moon as female?

Creating a poster poem

One of these poems is to be produced as a full colour poster which will
combine the poem with one or more illustrations. The poster will be
displayed in public places such as railway stations.

■ Decide which poem you think would be best as a poster and why.
■ Write an artwork brief for the poster. This is a short but clear description
of what you want the illustrator to do. Your description should help the
artist produce the right kind of illustration which will accurately and
sympathetically reflect the poem.

A25 *Rhyme and rhythm*

Rhyme

You can find rhyme in many places apart from poetry books.
People use rhyme in jokes, advertisers use it to sell products.

- Where else might you find rhymes being used? Look at the photographs on this page to help you.
- Why do people use rhyme and what does it do?

6 Catalogue

Cats sleep fat and walk thin.
Cats, when they sleep, slump;
When they wake, stretch and begin
Over, pulling their ribs in.
Cats walk thin.

Cats wait in a lump,
Jump in a streak,
Cats, when they jump, are sleek
As a grape slipping its skin –
They have technique.
Oh, cats don't creak.
They sneak.

Cats sleep fat.
They spread out comfort underneath them
Like a good mat,
As if they picked the place
And then sat,
You walk around one
As if he were the City Hall
After that.

If male,

17 City

What would my Grandma have said
If she could have seen the green
Where once the houses stood,
Last year with red-black brick
And rotten boards and broken glass?

Would she have loved new grass?
Or would she just have moaned
About the loss of foggy yesterday
Where she and Grandad used to play
With whips and spinning tops
Between old cobblestones and chased
Wild arrowed boys back home
Along the narrow alley ways?

John Kitching

Roses are red,
Violets are blue,
Most poems rhyme,
This one doesn't.

There are plenty of alternative versions of the above poem. Nearly all of
them rhyme. When you expect a rhyme and you don't find one, it sounds
wrong. When you expect a rhyme and it happens, there is a sense that the
verse has been completed. The rhyme at the end is sometimes what keeps
people reading on. Unusual rhymes can create humour or surprise or both.

There was a young woman called Maggie
Whose dog was enormous and shaggy;
The front end of him
Looked vicious and grim
But the tail end was friendly and waggy.

Rhyme schemes

Rhyme schemes are indicated in a fairly straightforward way in poems. The first line is called `a` and any lines that rhyme with it are also called `a`. When you come to a line that does not rhyme with it, it is called `b` and so are any lines that rhyme with it. This pattern simply continues until the end of the poem.

> `a` I've got a dog, thin as a rail,
> `a` He's got fleas all over his tail;
> `b` Every time his tail goes flop,
> `b` The fleas on the bottom hop to the top.

Practice

Work out the rhyme scheme for the short poem on page 82:
There was a young woman called Maggie.

Thinking

What rhymes can you think of that people might find in places other than a poetry book? Remember as many as you can that are suitable for repeating in a classroom and try to say where you heard them first.

A rhyme is for ...

Rhymes do all sorts of things. Here are some of the things that other people have claimed that rhymes do:

a Rhymes help to make an idea memorable.
b Rhymes can give a sharpness to what someone is saying.
c Rhymes are the glue that makes words stick together.
d Rhymes help to give a sense of completion.
e Rhymes help to hold a poem together.
f Rhymes help the flow of a poem.
g The pleasure with rhyme is in guessing what comes next.

1 Put the statements **a–g** in order of importance, with the one that best describes what rhymes do at the top.
2 Try to explain why you put the top two in those places.

The Heinemann English Programme 4 – Foundation

Rhythm

The effect of a rhyme is often emphasised by a regular rhythm. It's there in nursery rhymes and playground chants.

> Queenie, Queenie Caroline
> Dipped her hair in turpentine:
> Turpentine to make it shine,
> Queenie, Queenie Caroline.

The pattern here has a stressed sound (X) followed by an unstressed one (−).

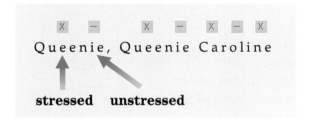

Patterns

Most words have a natural rhythm because some sounds in a word are stressed whilst others are not.

1 Work out which sound is **stressed** in these words. Write the word and put an X above it like this:

X
reader

joker   defender   performance
reflection   inspector

2 Work out which sounds are unstressed in these words. Mark them with a −

−
reader

trouble   average   disappear
interest   mystery

3 Work out which sounds are stressed and which are unstressed in the following words. Write the pattern down like this:

X   −   X   −
o v e r s h o o t i n g

writer   awake   disapprove
interest   director   protection
revolving   visible   bubble
battery

4 Write down the pattern of stressed and unstressed sounds in the rhyme *Queenie, Queenie Caroline*. Remember the first line has already been done for you above, which will help you with the pattern.

Metre

The rhythm of lines in a poem is called the **metre**. One of the most common patterns found in English poetry is an unstressed syllable followed by one that is stressed. A sound pattern is created that goes 'de dum, de dum, de dum, de dum' for perhaps four or five repetitions in a line.

The greatest skill in all the world I hear
Is making younger brothers disappear.

The pattern of stresses looks like this:

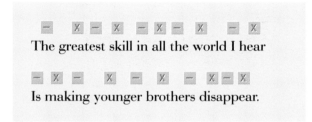

This kind of metre is called **iambic**. The pattern repeats five times in this case and iambic lines like these are called **iambic pentameters**. Of course, very few poems are entirely regular in their pattern and the exceptions to a pattern are often part of the interest: they make words and phrases stand out so the reader notices them.

Iambic sentences
Can you use this metre to create an iambic sentence? For example:
The teacher sat upon the biggest elephant.

Try to create:

- the **strangest** sentence you can
- the **funniest** sentence you can
- the **longest** sentence you can
- a sentence with a **rhyme**

each time using iambic metre.

Literary terms

metre
the rhythm of the line in a poem (the pattern of stressed and unstressed syllables)

iambic
'de-dum', an unstressed syllable followed by a stressed one, for example, 'begin'

iambic pentameter
a line with five 'de-dums', a ten syllable line with the pattern of an unstressed syllable followed by a stressed one.

Comparing two texts

In your examination you may be asked to compare two texts. Many people find this difficult; it is rather like trying to do two different things at the same time. These guidelines should help.

1 Read the first text carefully and think about it. You may find it helpful to read it a second time **before** you go on to the second.
2 Then do the same with the second text.
3 Look for common themes that help you to compare the two. There is a **checklist** of these at the bottom of the opposite page.

Do all these things before starting to answer any question(s) you have been set.

The two extracts that follow come from detective stories. In each of them, a private detective watches a house from a car. Read them and then look at the instructions on the opposite page.

A

I parked, aired out the convertible, had a drink from my bottle, and sat. I didn't know what I was waiting for, but something told me to wait. Another army of sluggish minutes dragged by.

Two cars came up the hill and went over the crest. It seemed to be a very quiet
5 street. At a little after six more bright lights bobbed through the driving rain. It was pitch-black by then. A car dragged to a stop in front of Geiger's house. The filaments of its lights glowed dimly and died. The door opened and a woman got out. A small slim woman in a vagabond hat and a transparent raincoat. She went in through the box maze. A bell rang faintly, light through the rain, a closing door, silence.
10 I reached a flash out of my car pocket and went down-grade and looked at the car. It was a Packard convertible, maroon or dark brown. The left window was down. I felt for the licence holder and poked light at it. The registration read: Carmen Sternwood, 3765 Alta Brea Crescent, West Hollywood. I went back to my car again and sat and sat. The top dripped on my knees and my stomach burned from the whisky. No more cars
15 came up the hill. No lights went on in the house before which I was parked. It seemed like a nice neighbourhood to have bad habits in.

At seven-twenty a single flash of hard white light shot out of Geiger's house like a wave of summer lightning. As the darkness folded back on it and ate it up a thin tinkling scream echoed out and lost itself among the rain-drenched trees. I was out of
20 the car and on my way before the echoes died.

vagabond hat: a felt hat with a broad brim which droops down over the face

B

I must have fallen asleep then, because when I woke up, my head was aching and my eyes burning, it was dark and the lights were on in Virginia's flat. If anything had happened I would have missed it, and I wondered what to do.

In the end I decided to stay where I was. It was only about eight, and I comforted myself with the reflection that if either of the two turned up, it was likely to be late.

A few hours passed, and a number of people went in and out of the block of flats but I spotted no one likely. Two or three people looked as if they might be visitors for Dick, but by midnight they had left.

I was thinking about leaving myself as one o'clock approached. The street was now deserted except for the occasional drunk, or the odd little group of young people in party clothes.

Suddenly a black custom-built car came round the corner and stopped in front of the flat. The front grille glowed with red spotlights and a string of amber lights winked on and off in the back window. As the car went past I had heard the beat of reggae music.

The driver got out, locked the door carefully and swaggered into the doorway of the building.

He was a bearded black man wearing a fawn three-piece suit with matching shoes, topped off by a brown and white woollen hat with a bobble on it.

I sat up. This looked an interesting prospect. He wasn't mixed race so he couldn't be Roy, but he could be connected in some way.

I got out of the car and stood closer to the doorway, but after fifteen minutes I went back. It was another hour before he came out, and then he was carrying a stereo.

He put it in the boot of his car and went back up. A few minutes later he came out again with a TV set. He made two more trips with a video machine and then a large suitcase, which he carried as if it was heavy.

It seemed that the couple was selling off the contents of the flat, and I wondered whether they'd decided to do a runner.

I crossed the road and came up behind the man just as he was closing the boot.

'Hey bro,' I said.

I wasn't sure how I was going to carry on the conversation but that was as far as I got.

He turned faster than I could move, and hit me in the stomach.

Checklist

Write down your answers to these questions.

Subject

1 What is the subject of each text? (In this case, what happens in the story of each one?)
2 In what ways are they similar in the way they treat the subject?
3 In what ways do they treat the subject differently?

Writing

4 What can you say about the **point of view** of each one? You can say whether a story is an 'I' story or a 'they' story. (See page 70 for information about *point of view*.)

5 Does each text follow a similar pattern? (For example, these two both end with a surprise – the scream, and the blow.)
6 Do they **sound** similar, or different? (Both these are 'I' stories, but what are the two speakers **like?**)
7 What else can you say about the writing of each one?

Your opinion

8 What do you think are the good points of each text and why?
9 Are there any bad points in either of them? If so, what are they and what are your reasons for saying so?

Punchlines

This is how the two extracts continue. Read them and
then follow the instructions on the opposite page.

A

There was no fear in the scream. It had a sound of half-pleasurable shock, an
accent of drunkenness, an overtone of pure idiocy. It was a nasty sound. It made me
think of men in white and barred windows and hard narrow cots with leather wrist
and ankle straps fastened to them. The Geiger hideaway was perfectly silent again
25 when I hit the gap in the hedge and dodged around the angle that masked the front
door. There was an iron ring in a lion's mouth for a knocker. I reached for it, I had hold
of it. At that exact instant, as if somebody had been waiting for the cue, three shots
boomed in the house. There was a sound that might have been a long harsh sigh.
Then a soft messy thump. And then rapid footsteps in the house – going away.
30 The door fronted on a narrow run, like a footbridge over a gully, that filled the gap
between the house wall and the edge of the bank. There was no porch, no solid
ground, no way to get around to the back. The back entrance was at the top of a flight
of wooden steps that rose from the alley-like street below. I knew this because I heard
a clatter of feet on the steps, going down. Then I heard the sudden roar of a starting
35 car. It faded swiftly into the distance.
I thought the sound was echoed by another car, but I wasn't sure. The house in
front of me was as silent as a vault. There wasn't any hurry. What was in there was in
there.
I straddled the fence at the side of the runway and leaned far out to the draped but
40 unscreened French window and tried to look in at the crack where the drapes came
together. I saw lamplight on a wall and one end of a bookcase. I got back on the
runway and took all of it and some of the hedge and gave the front door the heavy
shoulder. This was foolish. About the only part of a California house you can't put your
foot through is the front door. All it did was hurt my shoulder and make me mad. I
45 climbed over the railing again and kicked the French window in, used my hat for a
glove and pulled out most of the lower small pane of glass. I could now reach in and
draw a bolt that fastened the window to the sill. The rest was easy. There was no top
bolt. The catch gave. I climbed in and pulled the drapes off my face.
Neither of the two people in the room paid any attention to the way I came in,
50 although only one of them was dead.

Raymond Chandler: *The big sleep*

B

I saw the blow coming but I was falling to the pavement, gasping for breath and clutching at my midriff before I could react.

He walked unhurriedly away, and I heard the car door slam. Before I could get up he was driving away, the amber window lights blinking as if in mockery.

I got up, leaning on the wall, breathing deeply. There was no one around to see the incident, and for a moment I asked myself if it had really happened. I went back to the car and sat down, rubbing the spot.

The windows of the flat were still lit, and it struck me that the man's reaction must have meant that he had stolen the stuff, either from Virginia's flat or somewhere else.

I got out again and climbed the stairs, my legs feeling weak and rubbery. I rang on the bell. No answer. I rang again, then I noticed that the door moved a little when I pressed on the bell. It was still locked but when I pushed a thin crack appeared between the door and the frame. I pushed and listened. No sound, although the lights were on.

I rang again then pushed hard with my shoulder. All of a sudden the door sprang open with a bang.

I went in.

A light was on in the hallway and in the room beyond.

'Dick. Sally,' I called out.

No answer. I called out again and walked slowly into the room.

The couple were lying on the sofa. Dick was stretched out in a comfortable pose, while Sally lay with her head on his lap.

I called out their names again. They didn't move and I leaned forward and shook Dick, who collapsed sideways, his hand trailing over the side of the sofa on to the floor. I felt his pulse, then Sally's. I couldn't feel anything.

They had looked peaceful and relaxed but now I could see they were dead.

Mike Phillips: *Blood rights*

Comparing

Compare the two texts using the **Checklist** on page 87.

Writing

Now write a comparison of the two texts. You may find it helpful to use this plan:

1 **Introduction** (1 or 2 paragraphs)
   what each text is about – how they are similar – ways in which they are different.
2 **Writing** (1 or 2 paragraphs)
   how each writer tells the story – the storyteller and his personality – the way each story builds to a climax.
3 **Your opinion** (1 or 2 paragraphs)
   summing up what you think are the good and bad points of each text.

 TF You will find further practice for this unit using texts from other cultures and traditions in the Teacher's File.

Section B contents

Each unit in this section focuses on a specific area of your syllabus: poetry, prose (pre- and post-1900), drama, media and non-fiction. The units offer opportunities to develop the skills from section A, practise for exams and undertake coursework assignments.

Activities are categorised like this:

Preparation   The reading, thinking and note-making required before undertaking longer pieces of writing or talking in response to a text, topic or situation.

Practice   Activities which result in a 'product' – usually, but not always, an extended piece of writing. These can be used for exam practice.

Coursework   Longer writing activities which can produce material suitable for inclusion in a coursework folder.

STONE COLD

See:
A20 Character (p62)
A21 Action! (p66)
A22 Viewpoint (p70)

In *Stone cold*, a novel by Robert Swindells, Link is a homeless teenager living down and out in London.

So you pick your spot. Wherever it is (unless you're in a squat or a derelict house or something) it's going to have a floor of stone, tile, concrete or brick. In other words it's
5 going to be hard and cold. It might be a bit cramped, too – shop doorways often are. And remember, if it's winter you're going to be half frozen before you even start. Anyway you've got your place, and if you're lucky enough to
10 have a sleeping-bag you unroll it and get in.
   Settled for the night? Well maybe, maybe not. Remember my first night? The Scouser? 'Course you do. He kicked me out of my bedroom and pinched my watch. Well, that
15 sort of thing can happen any night, and there are worse things. You could be peed on by a drunk or a dog. Happens all the time – one man's bedroom is another man's lavatory. You might be spotted by a gang of lager louts
20 on the look-out for someone to maim. That happens all the time too, and if they get carried away you can end up dead. There are the guys who like young boys, who think because you're a dosser you'll do anything for
25 dosh, and there's the psycho who'll knife you for your pack.
   So, you lie listening. You bet you do. Footsteps. Voices. Breathing, even. Doesn't help you sleep.

Preparation

Questions

1 Which words show Link is speaking directly to the reader as if he were talking to a friend?
2 Pick out the three most effective details which you think make sleeping rough seem real. Why are they effective?
3 What dangers does Link face?
4 What order are they listed in?
5 Why do you think that he has chosen that order?

Then there's your bruises. What bruises? Try lying on a stone floor for half an hour. Just half an hour. You choose any position you fancy, and you won't find it comfy, I can tell you. You won't sleep unless you're dead drunk or zonked on downers. And if you are, and do, you're going to wake up with bruises on hips, shoulders, elbows, ankles, and knees – especially if you're a bit thin from not eating properly. And if you do that for six nights you'll feel like you fell out of a train. Try sleeping on concrete then.

And don't forget the cold. If you've ever tried dropping off to sleep with cold feet, even in bed you'll know it's impossible. You've got to warm up those feet, or lie awake. And in January, in a doorway, in wet trainers, it can be quite a struggle. And if you manage it, chances are you'll need to get up for a pee, and then it starts all over again.

And those are only some of the hassles. I haven't mentioned stomach cramps from hunger, headaches from the flu, toothache, fleas and lice. I haven't talked about homesickness, depression or despair. I haven't gone into how it feels to want a girl-friend when your circumstances make it virtually impossible for you to get one – how it feels to know you're a social outcast in fact, a non-person to whom every ordinary everyday activity is closed.

Robert Swindells: *Stone cold*

Assignment

A television advertisement is going to be made using the character of Link to warn teenagers against running away from home and telling them of some of the horrors they might face living rough in a big city.

You are the director writing a letter to the actor who will be playing the part of Link. In your letter you must make the following things clear:

1 Your ideas about what Link would wear, what he looks like, what his voice would be like, how he would stand, walk and so on.
2 What it is about the tone of voice Link uses, the things he says and the way he speaks which makes the audience feel he is a friend.
3 How Link makes the dangers he faces so vivid.
4 What Link is like as a person.

Use examples from the passage to support your ideas.

The Heinemann English Programme 4 – Foundation

Preparation

Questions

6 What does Link say or do in this section you have just read to make it seem as if he is really talking to you?
7 Link suffers a lot. Find the phrases which you think are the best in the passage you have just read at showing how much he is suffering. (For example, being bruised, cold, tired.)
8 Why do you think Link goes on to list all the things he says 'I haven't mentioned'?

TF There is an exam practice paper and mark scheme for this unit in the Teacher's File.

Shelter

Unfortunately not everyone feels kindly towards the homeless.
A man called Shelter believes he is doing a service to his country
by killing teenage street people. Naturally Robert Swindells
writes about him in a different way.

Three is a significant number. It
crops up in all sorts of places. Three
cheers. The Three Musketeers. If I
had three wishes. Three blind mice.
5 The Blessed Trinity. The three armed
services. The three little pigs. A
significant number.

 I have three recruits now. When I
had one I was a murderer, two, a
10 double murderer, and now that I've
got three I suppose I'm a mass
murderer – what the Yanks call a
serial killer. If they caught me now,
which they won't, they'd probably
15 make a film of me.

significant number: a number with an important meaning

The Three Musketeers: three soldiers who swore to always
help each other. They fought with swords (or muskets)
The Blessed Trinity: Christians believe in one God who
shows Himself in three ways: as God the Father, as Jesus Christ
who was born and lived on the earth, and as the Holy Spirit.
They call them The Blessed Trinity
recruits: new people in my team

Naturally, I've arranged them in the Army way – tallest on the left, shortest on the right and they look quite smart – especially now that I've cut their hair. I'll have to try to get them some boots, or at least proper shoes – something which will take a shine. At the moment they're all wearing
20   those manky trainer things.

Last night's bit of business – signing up recruit number three – gave me particular pleasure. You'll know why presently, but let me start at the beginning. It was about 20.00 hours and I'd just begun my nightly patrol. It was an unpleasant evening – wind and sleet – exactly the sort of evening
25   one needs in my line of work …

Robert Swindells: *Stone cold*

Practice

On the trail

You are a detective searching for this murderer. You have found this page from Shelter's diary and the three bodies it mentions.

You hope that a careful reading of what the murderer has written will give you some valuable clues.

What can you discover about Shelter from his diary?

You may find the following questions helpful. Make notes on your answers so that you can use them later on. Be sure to give reasons for your opinions.

1   What makes Shelter's diary hard to read? Look at the words he uses and the way he puts them together.
2   Does this way of writing tell you anything about his state of mind?
3   How has he treated the bodies and why does he call them 'recruits'?
4   What does he say which shows he is proud of what he does?
5   Can you find any words or phrases which suggest that Shelter thinks that what he is doing is good, or does he think it is evil?
6   As a detective what do you think of what Shelter is doing and how would you describe him?

Public Appeal

The police are going to appeal to the public on *Crimewatch* for help in tracking this man down. You have been chosen to appear on the programme to give all the information you have about Shelter. You are going to make a short statement, speaking directly to camera.

1   You have to show what Shelter is like by reading parts from the diary and explaining what they show about him. Make a list of the main points you need to include.
2   Check through the notes you made earlier. Make sure that you haven't missed out anything important.
3   Now write the script of what you will say.

The Heinemann English Programme 4 – Foundation

B2 LEARNING to *Swim*

See: ● **A4** Reading for detail (p14)
● **A5** Reading 'between the lines' (p16) ● **A26** Comparisons (p86)

The two extracts that follow both describe how the writer learned to swim. After each one there are questions to test your understanding. At the end there is a longer piece of writing to do.

A

Mr Meldrum was a plumber. He and Mrs Meldrum had produced three children, all boys: in descending order of age they were Gary, Neil and Craig. There was also an Alsatian dog called Ruth … All six of them lived in a house not much bigger than ours. Mr Meldrum wore a blue working singlet at all
5 times. He was regarded in the district as something of a gypsy. In fact he was simply the most original man for miles. He made hardly any money but there was more going on in his house than in anybody else's. He had turned all the boys into good swimmers. Gary was exceptionally good and got his picture in the papers for swimming a mile at the age of ten. Neil was a bit of a black sheep
10 and Craig was simply dense, but even they were encouraged in their interests. Neil was mad about stamps and Craig was held by Mr Meldrum to be a promising biologist. In fact Craig's biological studies consisted mainly of picking up privet grubs and eating them. He would also tuck into the occasional centipede. Mrs Meldrum's understandable hysteria at such moments would be
15 overwhelmed by Mr Meldrum's gusto. He was the first man I had ever met who had that. In short, he was a ready-made father figure.
   The Meldrums taught me to swim. Mr Meldrum, Gary and Neil took me down to the creek in the park. Reeds lined the banks and willows kissed the surface. The water was as brown as oxtail soup but Mr Meldrum said that any
20 water was clean if you could catch healthy fish in it. All the Meldrums could swim across the creek underwater. To me it seemed a fabulous distance. Gary showed me how to hold my breath and keep my eyes open underwater. I could see his hair floating. Inside an hour I was dog-paddling. Mr Meldrum threw his own boys up in the air to turn back somersaults. Then I rode on Gary's
25 shoulders, Neil rode on his father's and we had battles in the shallow water.
   That was just the start.

Clive James: *Unreliable memoirs*

Preparation

Write short answers to these questions.

Overview

1 What impression do you get of the Meldrums' family life?
2 How did Clive James learn to swim?

Close reading

3 The writer describes Mr Meldrum as a 'ready-made father figure'. What do we learn from the passage:
   ■ about how he treated his sons?
   ■ explaining why Clive James admired him?

B At the southern end of (Bondi) Beach stand Bondi Ocean Baths, dominated by the Bondi Icebergs' Club. Since 1929 the Icebergs have swum through the winter season, from the first Sunday in May to the last Sunday in September. To qualify for membership a prospective Iceberg must swim at least three out of four Sundays 'irrespective of the weather and with good humour … for five years'. There is a 90 per cent drop-out rate and the club is for men only.

Reg Clark was a Bondi Iceberg who swam through storms. His skin might have been the product of a tannery. Reg said little; his extraordinary power and grace in the water expressed all that he seemed to want to say. I was eight when Reg taught me to swim seriously. Unsparingly he drove me to his standard, for which I am grateful. With the sun barely up over Bondi Baths, and waves crashing against and over the sea wall, I swam lap upon lap with Reg walking along the wall beside me. He was mostly silent; then a familiar intonation would enter my sodden brain: 'Face down…neck down … reach out … reach out … reach out … Go!' I was a loyal member of Bondi Swimming Club and raced every Saturday over 50, 100, and 200 yards. Reg would sometimes be there, not speaking but moving his lips: 'Reach out … reach out.' When I came second to Murray Rose, who went on to win an Olympic gold medal, Reg was waiting at the finish. 'Wherejageto?' he said, almost smiling.

When the races were over my friend Pete and I would defy Big Norm, who blew the whistle of authority at the baths, and dive from the wall into the ocean. Waiting for a wave to cover the rocks below, plunging into it as it recedes, then grabbing a safety rope slung between the wall and the rocks, is a perilous ritual practised by generations of Bondi kids. I missed the rope once, was picked up by the undertow and despatched downward, spinning like a top. I re-emerged with the ocean in my head and gut and blood pouring from 'barnacle rash'. 'Get outta there with that blood,' bellowed Big Norm, 'or the sharks'll have yer!'

John Pilger: *A secret country*

Preparation

Write short answers to these questions.

First thoughts

1 How would you sum up the writer's attitude towards swimming?

Overview

2 How did Reg Clark teach him to swim well?
3 What does the last paragraph tell us about the writer?

Close reading

4 What kind of person was Reg Clark and what makes you think so?

Comparisons

1 Each of these texts describes a man whom the writer admired. What are the similarities and the differences between the two men? Use the answers you have already made to help you here – especially question 3 on page 97 and question 4 above.
2 Both texts describe learning to swim. Write a comparison of:
   - what happened
   - how it is described.

Your writing

1 Think of an adult who has influenced your own life. Write a description of him or her. Include one or two important events in your relationship.
2 Both writers describe with imagination and humour how they learned to swim. Think of a skill you have learned, and write an account of how you learned it.

TF You will find further practice for this unit using texts from other cultures and traditions in the Teacher's File.

B3 SO THAT'S A POEM, SO WHAT?

See: ● **A5** Reading 'between the lines' (p16) ● **A24** Metaphor (p79)

Free Coal

He was picking coal from a tip
When I passed his bent back.
His small daughter squatted
Beside a half filled sack,
5 Holding it against the slope
Of the dribbling slag.
The sky was younger then
And life was a bowl of shadows
In a valley of faded days,
10 And I was too young for the mask
Of depression which that man carried
On his thin, unemployed face.

Robert Morgan

Preparation

So that's a poem, so what?

It's often easier to talk and write about
stories than it is about poems. There are
more words to discuss. With a poem,
you are often asking the four key
questions opposite.

Of course, responding to poetry is
not as simple as working through a list
of questions. They are a starting point
for thinking. Look at how key questions
become thoughts, and develop into
further questions about *Free Coal*.

Key questions

1 What strikes me immediately about
the poem?
2 What lines stay in my mind and why?
3 What parts interest or puzzle me?
4 What do I feel about the poem as a
whole:

■ How successful do I think it is?
■ Which parts work particularly well?
■ Which parts fail?

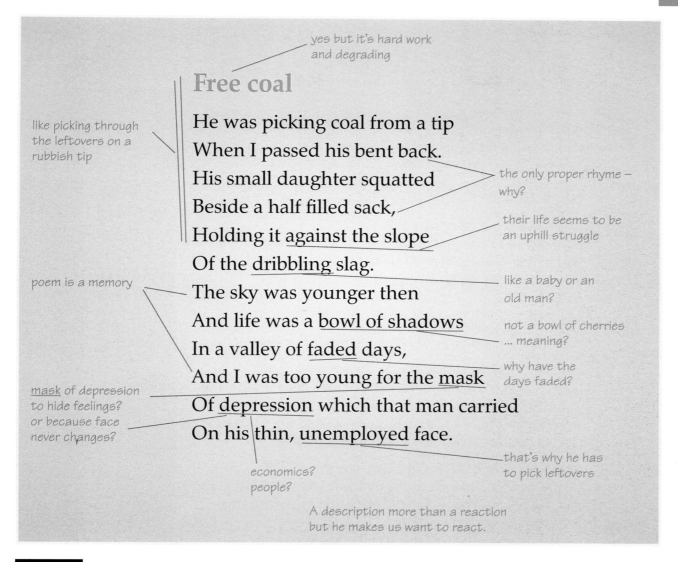

Free coal

yes but it's hard work
and degrading

like picking through
the leftovers on a
rubbish tip

He was picking coal from a tip
When I passed his bent back.
His small daughter squatted
Beside a half filled sack,
Holding it against the slope
Of the dribbling slag.

the only proper rhyme –
why?

their life seems to be
an uphill struggle

poem is a memory

The sky was younger then
And life was a bowl of shadows
In a valley of faded days,
And I was too young for the mask
Of depression which that man carried
On his thin, unemployed face.

like a baby or an
old man?

not a bowl of cherries
... meaning?

why have the
days faded?

mask of depression
to hide feelings?
or because face
never changes?

that's why he has
to pick leftovers

economics?
people?

A description more than a reaction
but he makes us want to react.

Practice

Coming to a sense of the poem

The notes around the poem show some clear responses.
There are still a lot of questions. How much can you help?

1 Read the comments around the poem, one by one. Write
down the ones that you think are useful. Add your own
thoughts to them.
2 Write a sentence or two about each of the **Key questions**.
3 Organise your answers into a paragraph or two which
gives your thoughts about the poem.

Heroines

Look at the poem below. Think and make notes about:

- what you understand
- what puzzles you
- what impression the poem creates for you.

Heroines

We are the terraced women
piled row upon row on the sagging, slipping hillsides of our lives
We tug reluctant children up slanting streets
the push chair wheels wedging in the ruts
5 breathless and bad tempered we shift the Tesco carrier bags from hand to hand
and stop to watch the town

the hill tops creep away like children playing games

our other children shriek against the schoolyard rails
'there's Mandy's mum, John's mum, Dave's mum, Kate's mum, Ceri's mother,
10   Tracey's mummy'
we wave with hands scarred by groceries and too much washing up
catching echoes as we pass of old wild games

after lunch, more bread and butter, tea
we dress in blue and white and pink and white checked overalls
15 and do the house and scrub the porch and sweep the street
and clean all the little terraces
up and down and up and down and up and down the hill

later, before the end-of-school bell rings
all the babies are asleep
20 Mandy's mum joins Ceri's mum across the street
running to avoid the rain
and Dave's mum and John's mum – the others too – stop for tea
and briefly we are wild women
girls with secrets, travellers, engineers, courtesans, and stars of fiction, films
25 plotting our escape like jail birds
terraced, tescoed prisoners rising from the household dust
like heroines.

Penny Windsor

Practice

Working through the poem in more detail

1 Where do the women live?
2 What fills up their time each day?
3 What do they look like?
4 What do they do when the babies are asleep?
5 Why do you think the poet describes the women as prisoners?
6 Why do you think 'up and down' is repeated in line 17?
7 Why do you think the poem is called *Heroines*?

Looking at the poem as a whole

Look at these statements.
Which three describe the poem best?
Put them in order: first, second, third.
Explain why you chose those three.

a The poem is about shopping and looking after children.
b The poem gives you a sense of how miserable life can be.
c The poem describes ordinary life for thousands of women.
d The poem expresses anger at the way women are trapped.
e The poem is about how daily routine wears people down.
f The poem is a humorous but sad look at ordinary life.
g The poem celebrates women who survive against the odds.

In the hot seat

What would the women say about their lives? Prepare the questions you would want to ask them. In pairs or groups, take turns at being one of the women and decide who gives the best impression of their lives.

Practice/Coursework

Your own writing

1 Try writing as if you were a mother or father waiting outside a primary school to pick up your young child at the end of the day. Try to give an impression of what life is like, just as Penny Windsor has done.
2 Look at the notes you have written and answers you have given to the questions about the poem. Think about what was said when you talked about it. Write about your response to it. You should include your answers to the **Key questions**:

■ What strikes me immediately about the poem?
■ What lines stay in my mind and why?
■ What parts interest or puzzle me?
■ What do I feel about the poem as a whole:

  – How successful do I think it is?
  – Which parts work particularly well?
  – Which parts fail?

B4 The *blind* man

See: ● **A5** Reading 'between the lines' (p16) ● **A13** Narrative (p38) ● **A20** Character (p62)

This unit contains a short story by Kate Chopin, an American writer who lived in St Louis in the southern part of the United States during the latter half of the nineteenth century. She wrote mainly during the 1880s and 1890s. It was a time of great change in the world she was observing.

- Industry and technology were growing fast.
- Towns were expanding.
- Poor people were getting poorer.
- Rich people were getting richer.
- Tensions were growing between rich and poor (which led to several strikes).
- Rich people were nervous about how safe their money was (because of stock market panics).
- There were worries about how people behaved to each other.

A man carrying a small red box in one hand walked slowly down the street. His old straw hat and faded garments looked as if the rain had often beaten upon them, and the sun had as many times dried them upon his person. He was not old, but he seemed feeble; and he walked
5 in the sun, along the blistering asphalt pavement. On the opposite side of the street there were trees that threw a thick and pleasant shade; people were all walking on that side. But the man did not know, for he was blind, and moreover he was stupid.

In the red box were lead pencils, which he was endeavouring to sell.
10 He carried no stick, but guided himself by trailing his foot along the stone copings or his hand along the iron railings. When he came to the steps of a house he would mount them. Sometimes, after reaching the door with great difficulty, he could not find the electric button, whereupon he would patiently descend and go his way. Some of the
15 iron gates were locked – their owners being away for the summer – and he would consume much time in striving to open them, which made little difference, as he had all the time there was at his disposal.

At times he succeeded in finding the electric button; but the man or maid who answered the bell needed no pencil, nor could they be
20 induced to disturb the mistress of the house about so small a thing.

garments: clothes

blistering asphalt: extremely hot tarmac

endeavouring: trying

stone copings: kerbstones

consume: use up
striving: making an effort
at his disposal: available

induced: persuaded

Preparation

Questions

1 What impression of the blind man do you get from the first paragraph?
2 Do you think the writer will be sympathetic to the blind man?
3 What do you think might happen to the blind man?

Picturing the blind man

Two different artists drew the pictures of the blind man on these two pages. As you read the rest of the story, try to work out which is the better picture and why.

The man had been out long and had walked very far, but had sold nothing. That morning someone who had finally grown tired of having him hanging around had equipped him with this box of pencils, and sent him out to make his living. Hunger, with sharp
25 fangs, was gnawing at his stomach and a consuming thirst parched his mouth and tortured him. The sun was broiling. He wore too much clothing – a vest and coat over his shirt. He might have removed these and carried them on his arm or thrown them away; but he did not think of it. A kind-hearted woman who saw him from
30 an upper window felt sorry for him, and wished that he would cross over into the shade.

    The man drifted into a side street, where there was a group of noisy, excited children at play. The colour of the box which he carried attracted them and they wanted to know what was in it. One
35 of them attempted to take it away from him. With the instinct to protect his own and his only means of sustenance, he resisted, shouted at the children and called them names. A policeman coming around the corner and seeing that he was the centre of a disturbance, jerked him violently around by the collar; but upon
40 perceiving that he was blind, considerately refrained from clubbing him and sent him on his way. He walked on in the sun.

consuming: overpowering
parched: made very dry
broiling: burning
vest: waistcoat

sustenance: making a living

perceiving: understanding
refrained: held back

During his aimless rambling he turned into a street where there were monster electric cars thundering up and down, clanging wild bells and literally shaking the ground beneath his
45 feet with their terrific impetus. He started to cross the street.

Then something happened – something horrible happened that made the women faint and the strongest men who saw it grow sick and dizzy. The motorman's lips were as gray as his face, and that was ashen gray; and he shook and staggered from
50 the superhuman effort he had put forth to stop his car.

Where could the crowds have come from so suddenly, as if by magic? Boys on the run, men and women tearing up on their wheels to see the sickening sight; doctors dashing up in buggies as if directed by Providence.

55 And the horror grew when the multitude recognized in the dead and mangled figure one of the wealthiest, most useful and most influential men of the town – a man noted for his prudence and foresight. How could such a terrible fate have overtaken him? He was hastening from his business house – for
60 he was late – to join his family, who were to start in an hour or two for their summer home on the Atlantic coast. In his hurry he did not perceive the other car coming from the opposite direction, and the common, harrowing thing was repeated.

The blind man did not know what the commotion was all
65 about. He had crossed the street, and there he was, stumbling on in the sun, trailing his foot along the coping.

Kate Chopin: *The blind man*

monster electric cars: trams

impetus: force

buggies: small horse-drawn carriages
Providence: God
multitude: crowd

prudence and foresight: carefulness and awareness of the future
hastening: hurrying

harrowing: very disturbing
commotion: noise and confusion

Practice

Witness

You are a journalist who happened to be present at the scene of the accident. You rush back to the newspaper office and write a report on what happened. Explain exactly what happened and describe the people you saw at the scene, including the blind man.

The Heinemann English Programme 4 – Foundation

Your own story

Try writing your own story about an outsider in which something unexpected happens. Plan it in four stages.

Stage one

Think about the kind of outsider you might write about. For example you might choose:

- someone with a disability – if so, what disability?
- someone who looks different – how?

Write notes on your ideas. Think about:

- What the person looks like and the clothes they wear.
- How the person feels about their situation and how they feel about other people.

Stage two

Think about what might happen in your story:

- will it be a particular thing that happens?
- will it be a slice of their normal life?
- what twist or surprise could there be?

Write notes on your ideas.

Stage three

A good story often makes people take a second look at something – especially an opinion or attitude they have always taken for granted. Think about how your story could challenge people's ideas and make them think again. You can do this by:

- a twist at the end of the story
- one of the characters being forced to change in some way.

Stage four

Write your story.

 There is an exam practice paper and mark scheme for this unit in the Teacher's File.

Question

How is the changing world which Kate Chopin experienced reflected in her story *The Blind Man*?

To answer this, you need to look back at the story and at page 104 and make notes about how the story describes:

- the poor
- the rich
- the way people behave
- the growing town, industry and technology.

B5 YOUNG PEOPLE AND DRINKING

See:
- **A2** Finding things (p8)
- **A4** Reading for detail (p14)
- **A15** Explanation (p46)
- **A16** Argument and persuasion (p49)

Teenage crime surge drink-related
New figures on vandalism and violence

Town centre ban 'huge success'
Proposal for alcohol-free streets countrywide

Young drinkers want 'high kick and quick buzz'
The 18-24 market consumes less but wants premium strength

YOUNG PEOPLE AND DRINKING

A GUIDE FOR PARENTS

Drinking too much alcohol can be a problem not only for the drinkers, but for society in general. The main text in this unit is a leaflet for parents, suggesting ways in which they can advise teenage sons and daughters about alcohol.

Make brief notes in response to the questions on the next three pages. The activities on the last page will need more detailed answers.

Make sure that you understand everything at each stage before moving on – ask, discuss, take the time to look up words you do not recognise.

INTRODUCTION

Being a parent can be rewarding and fulfilling. It can also be frustrating and, on occasions, painful.

5   An important responsibility of parents is to prepare their children to cope with the adult world.

Children have much to learn and they begin learning from a very early age. Schools play a
10 large role. Friends and relatives are important.

But, usually, it is parents who have the most important influence on their children.

To discuss some subjects with their children can be difficult for parents. Sex is one and illicit
15 drugs is another. Yet another is to do with drinking alcohol.

This is a guide to help you help your children to make sensible decisions about drinking and, if they choose to drink, to do so responsibly.

SETTING AN EXAMPLE

20 This pamphlet will help you to have sensible discussions with your children about drinking.

But remember, how much you drink and how you behave will have a big influence on them. For instance, do you set a good example to your 25 children about drinking and driving? You cannot expect them to respect you if you say one thing and then do another.

Talk to your children about drinking when you get the chance but don't try to frighten them 30 with scare stories. Children are very sharp and quick to spot exaggerations – especially when they might not want to believe them.

So be factual – your children will be better equipped to make sensible decisions about 35 drinking if they know the facts.

BASIC FACTS

Fact 1   In whatever form you drink it, alcohol has the same effect on your body.

Fact 2   Those who think that they will come to 40 no harm if they avoid spirits or that beers and ciders are always the weakest alcoholic drinks are quite wrong.

Preparation

Questions

1 Why has the leaflet been written?
2 Why is the behaviour of parents important?
3 According to the last sentence of the **Introduction** section and the last sentence of **Setting an example**, who will decide whether a child drinks or not? Is the leaflet right?
4 Fact 1 takes for granted that the effects of alcohol are generally known. What might these effects be?

Fact 3 A useful way of knowing how much alcohol you are drinking is to think in terms of units. 1 unit means a $^{1}/_{2}$ pint of standard beer or cider or 1 pub tot of spirits or $^{3}/_{4}$ of a glass of wine or 1 pub measure of fortified wine (sherry, port etc.). So the drinks illustrated below contain roughly the same amount of alcohol.

Fact 4 Different brands of an alcoholic drink may be quite different in strength. A strong beer or cider is sometimes twice as strong as the standard product.

Fact 5 All drinks have their strength shown on the label. This is indicated as a percentage (%) by volume and may appear as Alcohol x% vol, Alc x% vol or x% where x shows the actual percentage of alcohol in the container.

Fact 6 It is illegal to drink alcoholic drinks on licensed premises or buy them from an off-licence if you are under 18 years old. Beer may be taken in a pub with a meal if you are over 16 years old.

Fact 7 Despite this, research shows that 30% of young people between 16 and 18 drink regularly on licensed premises.

Fact 8 For a young person to pretend to be 18 isn't clever – this could result in the licensee losing his or her licence and livelihood.

Fact 9 Research shows that 44% of young people between 16 and 18 years have experienced hangovers.

Fact 10 The body burns up alcohol at the rate of 1 unit an hour (see Fact 3). No amount of exercise, fresh air, black coffee or 'quack' medicines can speed this up.

Fact 11 Driving skills are badly affected by alcohol – young people's more than adults'. The most sensible option if you are going to drive is not to drink.

Preparation

Questions

Facts 1–11

5 Which of these facts did you know already?

6 Did any of them come as a surprise to you?

7 Did you find any of them difficult to understand?

8 Can you suggest why young people's driving skills should be more affected by alcohol than an older person's?

IN THE HOME

Here are some simple, but very important, home rules:-

90 • If you drink in the home always stay in control – make it a natural and enjoyable part of your lifestyle;

• Don't encourage your children to drink – if they want a taste of what you are drinking, give
95 them a sip but don't make a big issue out of it. Remember it is illegal to give alcohol to a child under 5 years old;

• Never let teenagers drink in your home unless a responsible adult is present. An unsupervised
100 party is asking for trouble – make sure plenty of non-alcoholic drinks are available;

• Don't leave alcohol lying around – keep it in a secure cupboard or drinking cabinet;

• Give your children the facts about alcohol and
105 drinking. Be natural and open. Don't preach or moralise. There is no ideal age to begin giving information and advice but it should be before the teenage years;

• Stay up and greet your child when he or she comes home – this makes it obvious that you 110 are concerned – take an interest in where they are going or where they have been.

COPING WITH TROUBLE

If your teenage son or daughter comes home 115 drunk don't overreact but use this as an opportunity, when he or she is over it, to have a straight talk. Don't preach or moralise – be calm and reasonable.

THE MAIN AIM

Always try to help your children to make sen- 120 sible decisions about drinking. This means, if they choose to drink, respecting the law and always staying in control. Try to prevent drinking problems before they occur.

The Portman Group:
Young people and drinking

Preparation

Questions

9a 'Don't preach or moralise' is used twice on this page. Choose the explanation below which you think is nearest in meaning:

■ don't say, 'It serves you right!'
■ don't say that drinking is wrong
■ don't be secretive
■ don't say, 'You should know better!'

9b Why do you think this phrase is used twice?

10 This last page consists of a number of pieces of advice to parents. Which do you consider to be the most valuable? Are there any which you think are so obvious as to be unnecessary? Explain your answer.

Practice
What do you think?

1 Look at the cartoons on this page. Should people be encouraged to think of drinking and drink-related problems as amusing?
2 Discuss the laws, as you know them, regarding alcohol and young people. Are there any laws with which you agree, or disagree, strongly? Can you suggest improvements to the laws as they stand?

Conversation

In **Coping with trouble** it is suggested that father or mother should have a straight talk with their son or daughter. What would this 'straight' talking be? In the form of a script, write the conversation between child and parent as you think it would happen.

Practice/Coursework
A guide for parents?

Thinking points

This leaflet is produced by the Portman Group which represents the 'drinks industry'.

"I suppose that dog's over eighteen?"

Make notes on your opinions about these questions:

1 Does this surprise you?
2 Can you suggest why breweries and distilleries would do this?
3 Do you think that a different organisation (such as the police) should to be responsible for such a leaflet?
4 How useful do you think this guide will be for parents? Think about:

- **what** the leaflet says
- **how** it says it
- the **layout** and **design** of the leaflet.

Write

Now use the ideas you have discussed as the basis for a piece of writing about the leaflet. Explain what you think are the good and bad points about it.

The Heinemann English Programme 4 – Foundation

B6 Badger

See: ● **A11** Making notes: why? (p34) ● **A12** Making notes: how? (p36)
● **A26** Comparing two texts (p86)

Before someone even reads a poem, they may have some fixed ideas about it. Perhaps the title interests them or puts them off so that they expect to be entertained or bored. Once anyone has an idea in their head it is very hard to change it. Before comparing the following two poems on badgers:

- think about what you know and how you feel about the animals
- think about your reactions to the illustrations on these two pages
- think about what you might expect in a poem about badgers.

Harmless they call him, a lovable nocturnal thing,
a family man spending daylight in his deep sett,
He has an old reputation for remaining aloof.
I thought he stuffed himself on insects and roots,
5 a fallen egg, a few mice, nothing his own size.
But from a cable-drum he came sniffing for our buck
after dark, baiting him and scratching at the mesh,
then deadly serious one night with his big jaws
and his bone-crushing molars rampant.
10 He wanted much more than a boring vegetable dish.

Grizzled snouter with the claws and thick white stripe,
he scooped a hole under the boxwood hutch,
splintered the floor with his ramming head
and then clambered up and through it.
15 Our poor young rabbit must have died of fright
but not before the badger minced him
into string and red slippery pulp.
That lovable thing left a smear of blood and droppings
on a mile-long strip of hutch and run
20 before a smallholder blew his head off.

John Tripp

nocturnal: awake at night
sett: underground home
aloof: apart, not involved
buck: male rabbit

molars: teeth

grizzled: streaked with grey
snouter: animal with long nose

smallholder: person with a small-sized farm

B6 Badger

114

Preparation

First reactions

Make notes about your first reactions to the poem. Include:

- your thoughts about the poem as a whole
- your thoughts about individual parts of the poem that impressed you.

Second thoughts

Look again at the poem and make notes about:

1 words that are effective
2 the words and phrases that help you to picture the badger
3 the feelings you have as you read the poem
4 the overall impact the poem has.

Think about these things:

- the ideas and images the poet originally had of a badger
- what changed his mind
- words that give a sense of the badger's violence
- the way the poem ends
- what happens in each stanza (verse)
- anything else that strikes you.

Tips for making notes

Use **phrases** or **short sentences**:

- to capture your thoughts and ideas
- in no particular order
- which need not be 'posh'
- which need to be clear enough to be understood later,

for example:

'before the badger minced him'

– like use of mince

– gives sense of violence

– badger is like butcher

– rabbit is just a meal to him

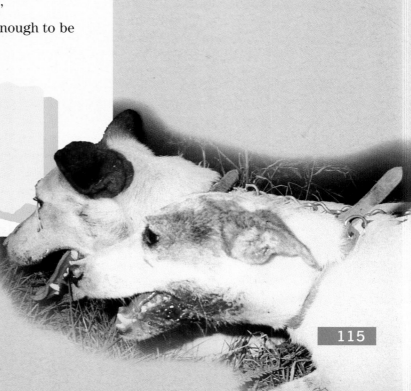

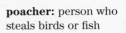

The badger

When midnight comes a host of dogs and men
Go out and track the badger to his den,
And put a sack within the hole, and lie
Till the old grunting badger passes by.

5   He comes and hears – they let the strongest loose.
The old fox hears the noise and drops the goose.
The poacher shoots and hurries from the cry,
And the old hare half wounded buzzes by.
They get a forked stick to bear him down

10 And clap the dogs and take him to the town,
And bait him all the day with many dogs,
And laugh and shout and fright the scampering hogs
He runs along and bites at all he meets:
They shout and hollo down the noisy streets.

15 He turns about to face the loud uproar
And drives the rebels to their very door.
The frequent stone is hurled where'er they go;
When badgers fight, then everyone's a foe.
The dogs are clapped and urged to join the fray;

20 The badger turns and drives them all away.
Though scarcely half as big, demure and small,
He fights with dogs for hours and beats them all.
The heavy mastiff, savage in the fray,
Lies down and licks his feet and turns away.

25 The bulldog knows his match and waxes cold,
The badger grins and never leaves his hold.
He drives the crowd and follows at their heels
And bites them through – the drunkard swears and reels.

The frighted women take the boys away,

30 The blackguard laughs and hurries on the fray.
He tries to reach the woods, an awkward race,
But sticks and cudgels quickly stop the chase.
He turns again and drives the noisy crowd
And beats the many dogs in noises loud.

35 He drives away and beats them every one,
And then they loose them all and set them on.
He falls as dead and kicked by dogs and men,
Then starts and grins and drives the crowd again;
Till kicked and torn and beaten out he lies

40 And leaves his hold and cackles, groans, and dies.

John Clare

poacher: person who steals birds or fish

bear: pin

bait: torment
scampering hogs: running pigs

hollo: call loudly

uproar: great noise
drives: pushes back (or forward)

foe: enemy
fray: fight

demure: calm

waxes: grows

reels: staggers

frighted: frightened
blackguard: rogue, villain
awkward: difficult
cudgels: short heavy clubs

cackles: makes a harsh broken noise

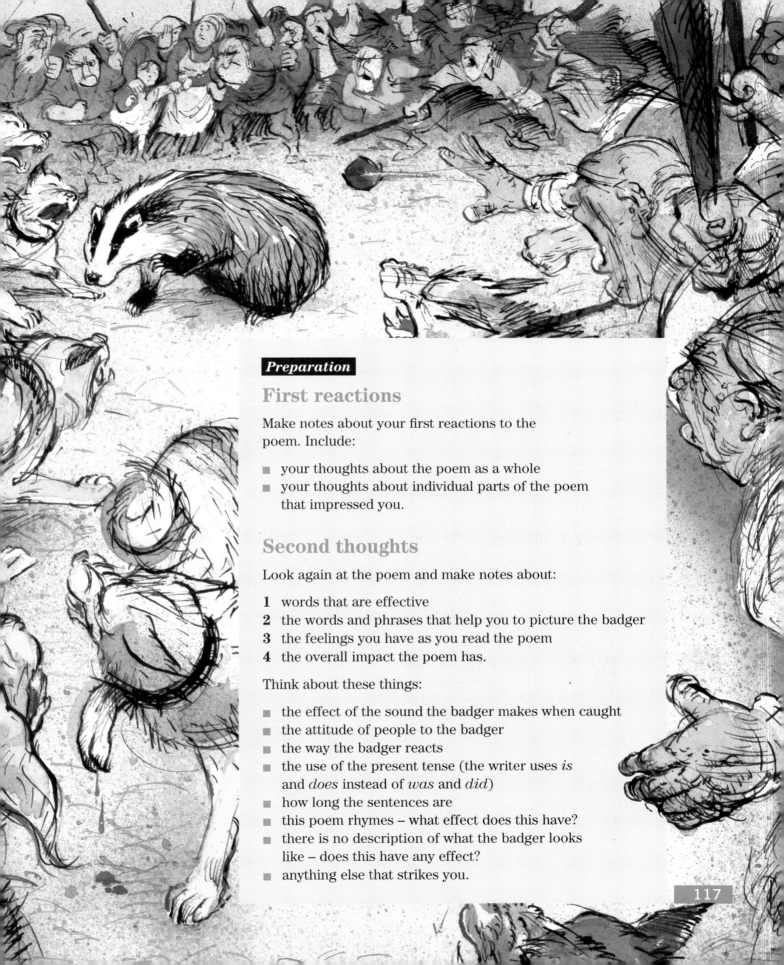

First reactions

Make notes about your first reactions to the poem. Include:

- your thoughts about the poem as a whole
- your thoughts about individual parts of the poem that impressed you.

Second thoughts

Look again at the poem and make notes about:

1 words that are effective
2 the words and phrases that help you to picture the badger
3 the feelings you have as you read the poem
4 the overall impact the poem has.

Think about these things:

- the effect of the sound the badger makes when caught
- the attitude of people to the badger
- the way the badger reacts
- the use of the present tense (the writer uses *is* and *does* instead of *was* and *did*)
- how long the sentences are
- this poem rhymes – what effect does this have?
- there is no description of what the badger looks like – does this have any effect?
- anything else that strikes you.

Third step: summing up each poem

What is special or distinctive about each of the two poems?
Write two or three sentences about each poem.
Some points to consider are:

John Tripp's poem

- the horror
- his change of opinion
- the details of what a badger does.

John Clare's poem

- badger baiting as sport
- the determination of the badger
- the attitude of the crowd.

Fourth step: comparisons

What are the main differences and similarities between the poems?
Think about:

- the strength of a badger as you see it in each poem
- what a badger does and what is done to a badger
- the end of each poem
- the scenes pictured in each poem
- the attitude of each poet to the badger and what happens in each poem.

Practice

Writing

Write up your comparison of the two poems.
The following structure may be useful:

a First paragraph saying what is special about each poem.
b Paragraphs about the detail in the first poem.
c Paragraphs about the detail in the second poem.
d Final paragraphs:

- about the way the poems are similar
- about the way the poems are different
- summing up what you think about them as a whole.

Remember to quote from the poems to support what you say.

TF	There is an exam practice paper and mark scheme for this unit in the Teacher's File.

B7 *On the look-out*

See: ● **A5** Reading 'between the lines' (p16) ● **A20** Character (p62) ● **A21** Action! (p66)

Questions

This picture shows the scene at the beginning of a story.

1 When and where do you think it is set?
2 What are your first impressions of the two characters?
3 What do you think they are doing?

This is the beginning of *Our Mutual Friend,* a novel by Charles Dickens. If you read it slowly, pausing slightly at the commas, you will find the long sentences easier to follow.

In these times of ours, a boat of dirty and disreputable appearance, with two figures in it, floated on the Thames, between Southwark Bridge and London Bridge, as an autumn evening was closing in.

5   The figures in this boat were those of a strong man with ragged grizzled hair and a sun-browned face, and a dark girl of nineteen or twenty, sufficiently like him to be recognisable as his daughter. The girl rowed, pulling a pair of sculls very easily; the man, with the rudder-lines slack in his hands, and his hands loose in his waistband, kept an eager look-out. She watched his face as earnestly as she watched the river. But, in the intensity of her look, there
10 was a touch of dread or horror.

> **disreputable**: not respectable, untidy
> **grizzled**: streaked with grey
> **sculls**: oars
> **rudder-lines**: thin ropes with which he could steer the boat
> **slack**: loose

Preparation

After you have read each section of the story write down your answers to the questions that follow. You don't need to write complete sentences.

Questions

1 Where does this scene take place? (lines 1–3)
2 When does it take place? (lines 1–3)
3 What does the man look like? (lines 4–5)
4 What does the girl look like? (lines 5–6, 9–10)
5 What is the girl doing? (lines 6–7, 8–9)
6 What is the man doing? (lines 7–8)

Your thoughts

7 What questions does this first section make you want to ask?
8 What do you think might happen next?

Watching

This boat and the two figures in it obviously were doing something that they often did, and were seeking what they often sought. Half savage as the man showed, with such dress as he wore seeming to be made out of the mud that begrimed his boat, still there was a business-like usage in his steady gaze. So with every lithe action of the girl, with every turn of her wrist, perhaps most of all with her look of dread and horror; they were things of usage.

'Keep her out, Lizzie. Tide runs strong here. Keep her well afore the sweep of it.'

Trusting to the girl's skill and making no use of the rudder, he eyed the coming tide with an absorbed attention. So the girl eyed him. But a slant of light from the setting sun glanced into the bottom of the boat, and, touching a rotten stain there which bore some resemblance to the outline of a muffled human form, coloured it as though with diluted blood. This caught the girl's eye, and she shivered.

'What ails you?' said the man, immediately aware of it, though so intent on the advancing waters; 'I see nothing afloat.'

The red light was gone, the shudder was gone, and his gaze, which had come back to the boat for a moment, travelled away again. Wheresoever the strong tide met with an impediment, his gaze paused for an instant. At every mooring chain and rope, at every stationary boat or barge that split the current into a broad-arrow-head, at the floating logs of timber lashed together lying off certain wharves, his shining eyes darted a hungry look.

begrimed: dirtied
there was a business-like usage in his steady gaze: the way he watched showed that he was doing his regular work
lithe: skilful and easy
usage: habit
afore the sweep of it: well out in the middle, away from where the current pushes towards the bank
impediment: obstruction

Preparation

Questions

1 What new information do we learn about the man and the girl?
2 What does each do in this section?
3 Look carefully at lines 19–22. Why do you think the girl shivers?
4 Look at lines 26–29. What do you think he is looking for – in these particular places?

Your thoughts

5 Look back at the questions you wrote down before (page 120, question 7). Does this section of the story answer any of them?
6 Does this section make you want to ask any more questions? If so, write them down.
7 What do you think might happen next?

The find

30 After a darkening hour or so, suddenly the rudder-lines tightened in his hold, and he steered hard towards the Surrey shore.

Always watching his face, the girl instantly answered to the action in her sculling; presently the boat swung round, quivered as from a sudden jerk, and the upper half of the man was stretched out over the stern. The girl pulled the hood of a cloak she

35 wore, over her head and over her face, and, looking backward, kept the boat in that direction going before the tide. Until now, the boat had barely held her own; but now, the banks had changed swiftly, and the deepening shadows and the kindling lights of London Bridge were passed, and the tiers of shipping lay on either hand.

It was not until now that the upper half of the man came back into the boat. His

40 arms were wet and dirty, and he washed them over the side. In his right hand he held something, and he washed that in the river too. It was money. He chinked it once, and he blew upon it once, and he spat upon it once, – 'for luck,' he hoarsely said – before he put it in his pocket.

presently: straightaway
kindling lights: lights that are just being lit
tiers: series of rows

Charles Dickens: *Our mutual friend*

Preparation

Questions

1 What new information do we learn about the man?
2 What does he do in this section?
3 What new information do we learn about the girl?
4 What does she do in this section?

Your thoughts

5 Look back at the questions you have written down so far. How many of them have now been answered?
6 Can you guess the answers to the others?
7 How do you think the story might continue?

The mystery

Think about all three sections that you have now read. The mystery of what the father is looking for is solved by the end of the chapter – it is money.

Why do you think the daughter is horrified by what they are doing? Where has the money come from?

Practice

Television producer

You have been asked to produce a television adaptation of this story.

1 You have to tell the actors playing the father and daughter what they are like.
   Write a description of:
   ■ what they look like
   ■ how they move and speak
   ■ their personalities
   ■ how they behave towards each other.
2 You have to meet the scriptwriter. Write a description of:
   ■ the place and time in which the story is set
   ■ the atmosphere
   ■ key pictures or shots that you want to include and why.

Coursework

Your writing

Write a short story on one of these titles.

■ 'We shouldn't have kept the money'
■ The search
■ The trouble with a fiver

B8 image breakers

See:
- **A6** Fact and opinion (p20)
- **A8** Why write? (p26)
- **A10** Tone and formality (p31)
- **A16** Argument and persausion (p49)
- **A26** Comparing two texts (p86)

Look at any collection of family photos and you can soon see how fashions change. Think for a moment about what is in and out of fashion in these areas:

- clothes
- shoes
- music
- hairstyles

One of the most important influences in making something popular is advertising. But how do you make something fashionable? And what do you do if you are asked to advertise something that is clearly unfashionable?

The advertising agency that was given the job of re-launching Skoda cars had a massive problem: the cars had been the subject of jokes for as long as anyone could remember.

Question: *What do you call a sewing machine on wheels?*
Answer: *A Skoda.*

1 What cars can you think of that have an image problem?
2 Why do some cars have an image problem?
3 How would you have tried to improve Skoda's image?

What to do

Study the advertisement for Skoda on the next pages. The questions about the advertisement follow on page 126.

The Heinemann English Programme 4 – Foundation

Before we changed the car, we changed the company.

A car can tell you a lot about the company that made it.

When a company changes, the changes are visible in the cars that they make. At Skoda, over the past four years, we have changed more than any car maker in the world.

We've had to look long and hard at what we've been getting right, and what we've been getting wrong.

The good news.

People who buy our cars, like our cars. We've been getting the basics right. Price. Reliability. Engineering. And in Europe's leading customer satisfaction audit, J.D. Power*, Skoda beats the likes of BMW, Rover and Ford.

People who knew about cars, knew our history. For the first half of the century we were one of the world's greatest marques. When we built Hispano-Suizas, they were the most elegant cars on the road. When the cold war started, that all stopped. And the years of isolation took their toll.

The other news.

What we were getting wrong was, basically, everything else.

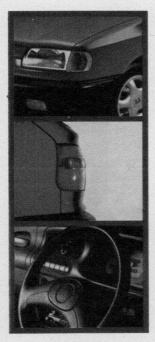

Volkswagen Group

We were too "inward-looking". We made the cars we wanted to make, rather than the cars most customers wanted. So, our cars have never had a "fashionable" image.

Conclusion: we had good people, but were using them in the wrong way. It had to change. It wasn't easy. It never is.

The change.

Volkswagen invested a huge amount of cash and expertise. We revolutionised our quality control systems. Totally revised our design processes. Everything was scrutinised by Volkswagen, everything.

We turned the company around.

The evidence.

You can see these changes in our new car, the Felicia. It's not what you'd expect from a Skoda.

It doesn't look the way you'd expect a Skoda to look. It doesn't feel the way you'd expect a Skoda to feel.

But it still gives you what Skoda always did: more car for less money.

We heard the criticisms. We changed our company. We changed our cars. Now, are you open enough to change your mind?

We've changed the car. Can you change your mind?

For a full information pack about the new Felicia, call 0345 745745. We'll also tell you where to find your nearest Skoda dealer.

*April 1995.

What the advertisement is trying to do

Answer these questions in your own words as far as possible.

Paragraphs 1 – 3 of the advertisement.

1 What have Skoda been doing?

Section headed 'The good news'

2 What has been working well for Skoda?

3 How does this section try to impress you?

Look at what it says about the company's history.

Section headed 'The other news'

4 What was the company's main fault?

5 Why is this section not called 'The bad news'?

Section called 'The change'

6 Think about the words and phrases that give an impression of great change. For example:

> 'huge amount of cash and expertise' –
> the word 'huge' is there to give an impression of the size of the effort being made to change.

Choose two other words or phrases that suggest change and explain why you have chosen them.

Section headed 'The evidence'

7 Why might someone who needs a car be tempted to go and look at a Skoda?

Writing: Is this a good advertisement?

Look at the advertisement as a whole including the photographs. Write your opinion about it: is it successful or not? You should include comments on these points:

- what attracts your attention
- the layout (including the headlines and sub-headings)
- the pictures
- things that are repeated
- what you learn about Skoda
- whether you are convinced by the writing
- whom the advertisement might appeal to.

New schools for old

Every time there is a special event for parents, most teachers have one complaint: 'We never see the parents we really wanted to see.'

There are plenty of parents who do not enjoy stepping inside schools if they can avoid it. Their own schooldays have put them off for life! When you hear some of the stories of what used to go on in school, you can hardly blame them. (But can you believe the stories that parents tell you?)

Your school wants to run an open day or evening that is especially directed at parents who do not normally step inside the school gate. It needs good ideas and good publicity.

Assignment

The photographs on these pages show some of the changes that have taken place in schools.

You have been asked to prepare a leaflet advertising a Parents' Open Evening for your school. Your task is to produce a piece of advertising that makes parents feel that schools are different places today than they were 20 or 30 years ago. There are three stages to go through before you write the text of your leaflet. As you go through each one **make notes** of what you find out or decide.

1 Research

Talk to your parents and other people of your parents' age.
Here are five basic questions that you can use as a starting point:

1 What subjects did you do in school?
2 What were the teachers like?
3 What was discipline like?

4 What activities took place in a lesson?
   - teacher talk?   - group work?
   - copying notes?   - learning by heart?
5 How did pupils behave to each other?

A lot has changed

These notes were made by one teacher who was a pupil in the 1960s:

- Teachers dictated notes and you just wrote them down – sometimes you thought your hand was going to fall off.
- Some teachers hated biros (ballpoint pens) so you were forced to use fountain pens and then got into trouble for the splodges they created.
- Lots of us went to single sex schools – the opposite sex was something you went to look at through the railings of another school!
- There wasn't much practical work and there was even less opportunity for discussion.
- Both boys and girls got caned but I reckon the boys got it a lot more than the girls.
- Teachers can be boring now but they were even more boring then – some of them thought it didn't matter how they presented things and they had no sense of humour at all (but a few were brilliant!).
- There were so many silly little rules that didn't seem worth it, like having to wear your school cap all the way home.
- If you got bullied, that was just tough luck ... there was no one to talk to about it.

2 Audience

- What puts people off school?
- What is there in your school that you like?
- What do you think might interest your parents?
- How might an open day or evening be made more attractive to parents?

3 Purpose

Think about these questions:

- How will you sell the evening?

  concentrate on new developments?
  compare old and new?

- What details will make your publicity interesting to your audience?

  eye-catching headlines?
  quotes from parents?
  quotes from teachers?
  quotes from students?

- How can photographs help?

4 Writing

- Look at all the notes you have made. Use the material to work out:

  – **what** you want to include
  – the order in which you want to say things.

- Now write your leaflet.

since you were at school

More Than Just a Story

See: ● **A25** Rhyme and rhythm (p82) ● **A26** Comparing two texts (p86)

In the fourteenth century poets wrote and sang ballads.

A ballad is a poem which tells a story and has a very strong pattern of rhythm and rhyme. It usually tells a story about love, death, betrayal (being cheated by a lover who is unfaithful), or similar themes. In many ways ballads are like the song lyrics you find in some pop songs.

Ballads were so popular and effective that people still write them today.

This unit contains two modern ballads by Charles Causley. As you read the first one look for the story line and do not worry if you do not understand all the details straight away.

Lord Lovelace

LORD LOVELACE rode home from the wars,
His wounds were black as ice,
While overhead the winter sun
Hung out its pale device.

device: the picture or sign on a knight's banner (flag) and shield showing who he is. In the poem the sun is showing its 'pale device' because it is winter

5 The lance was tattered in his hand,
  Sundered his axe and blade,
  And in a bloody coat of war
  Lord Lovelace was arrayed.

lance: spear
sundered: broken

  And he was sick and he was sore
10 But never sad was he,
  And whistled bright as any bird
  Upon an April tree.

  'Soon, soon,' he cried, 'at Lovelace Hall
  Fair Ellen I shall greet,
15 And she with loving heart and hand
  Will make my sharp wounds sweet.

  And Young Jehan the serving-man
  Will bring the wine and bread,
  And with a yellow link will light
20 Us to the bridal bed.'

  But when he got to Lovelace Hall
  Burned were both the wall and stack,
  And in the stinking moat the tower
  Had tumbled on its back.

25 And none welcomed Lord Lovelace home
  Within the castle shell,
  And ravaged was the land about
  That Lord Lovelace knew well.

  Long in his stirrups Lovelace stood
30 Before his broken door,
  And slowly rode he down the hill
  Back to the bitter war.

  Nor mercy showed he from that day,
  Nor tear fell from his eye,
35 And rich and poor both fearful were
  When Black Lovelace rode by.

  This tale is true that now I tell
  To woman and to man,
  As Fair Ellen is my wife's name
40 And mine is Young Jehan.

Charles Causley

The Heinemann English Programme 4 – Foundation

What is the story?

Now that you have read the poem here are ten sentences which you need to put in the right order. There is one sentence for each verse. Put the sentences in the right order and copy them out and you will have written out the story of the poem.

1 When I, Lovelace, arrive home at Lovelace Hall, Young Jehan will feed us, and then my beloved and I will go to bed.
2 Lovelace was feeling ill and tired after all the fighting he had done, but he whistled cheerfully.
3 Lovelace was carrying his weapons and wearing blood stained clothing while he travelled.
4 Lovelace stood and looked long and hard at the ruins of his home and slowly rode away.
5 No one was there to welcome him and everywhere he looked was destroyed.
6 Since then Lovelace has changed into a hard, frightening man now nicknamed Black Lovelace.
7 This is a true story I am telling you, for I am Young Jehan and my wife is Ellen.
8 In the winter Lord Lovelace rode home from the wars.
9 His home, Lovelace Hall, was burned and ruined.
10 Lord Lovelace was cheerful because he was looking forward to seeing his beloved Ellen again.

What happens in the end?

Lord Lovelace is changed by what happens to him. He will never be the same person again.

1 **How** does the poem make it clear to us that he has changed?
2 **In what ways** does he change?
3 **Why** do you think he changed?
4 **What words or phrases** explain the change?

Looking at the details

One of the main ideas in a ballad is death. Look carefully at the first verse.

1 What time of year does it describe?
2 Lord Lovelace's wounds are '**black** as **ice**'. He is coming home in the '**winter** sun' which 'Hung out its **pale** device.' What have these details got to do with death?
3 What other images (word pictures) in the poem help to get across the idea of death?

What is the ballad about?

Say whether these statements are true or false and find sentences from the poem to support your answers.

A The poem is about love.
B The poem is about a lover being unfaithful.
C The poem is about death.

Ballad Of The Faithless Wife

Carry her down to the river
Carry her down to the sea
Let the bully-boys stare at her braided hair
But never a glance from me.

5 Down by the writhing water
Down by the innocent sand
They laid my bride by the toiling tide
A stone in her rifled hand.

Under the dainty eagle
10 Under the ravening dove
Under a high and healthy sky
I waited for my love.

Off she ran with a soldier
Tall as a summer tree,
15 Soft as a mouse he came to my house
And stole my love from me.

O splintered were all the windows
And broken all the chairs
War like a knife ran through my life
20 And the blood ran down the stairs.

Loud on the singing morning
I heard the mad birds rise
Safe from harm to the sun's alarm
As the sound of fighting dies.

25 I would hang my harp on the branches
And weep all through the day
But stranger, see! The wounded tree
Has burned itself away.

False O false was my lover
30 Dead on the diamond shore
White as a fleece, for her name was Peace
And the soldier's name was War.

Charles Causley

rifled: having had
everything stolen from it

ravening: taking
everything away by force

1 What is the story?

Re-read the poem and then put the eight sentences in the box in the right order to tell the story of the ballad.

1 She ran off with a soldier who came to my house.
2 They laid my beloved in the water with a stone in her hand.
3 I would mourn for her but I can't.
4 The windows and chairs in my house were smashed in a bloody fight.
5 Once I waited happily for my love.
6 The woman is being carried down to the water's edge by men who can admire her beauty but I cannot bear to look at her.
7 The fighting frightened the birds and I heard their singing as they flew away.
8 My lover was false to me, and she died, but our story is just like peace being destroyed by war.

2 Looking at the details

Look at the last verse:

> False O false was my lover
> Dead on the diamond shore
> White as a fleece, for her name was Peace
> And the soldier's name was War.

Think about these questions to see if you can understand any more about the details in this verse.

1 Where might the dead lover have gone to, and why would that place be described as having a 'diamond shore'?
2 A dead person's skin would obviously be white but now you know the dead woman's name you need to think some more. Why might the idea of Peace be described as 'White'?

3 What is the ballad about?

1 Which of the three main ballad ideas does this poem deal with:

- Love?
- Death?
- Betrayal?

2 Find some lines in the poem to support your opinion.

4 Assignment

Write a comparison of the ballads.

To help you, follow these points. For each point, write first about one ballad then about the other. At the end of each point, decide whether there are any similarities or differences between what you have said about each ballad and if there are, explain them.

1 Write one or two paragraphs about each poem explaining the story.
2 Explain what you think each poem is about. Use the notes you made on **What is the poem about?** to help you.
3 Explain which details (words or images) you find most effective in each poem.
4 Finish your piece of writing by giving your response to the two poems. What did you like about each one? Were there things you did not like?

| TF | There is an exam practice paper and mark scheme for this unit in the Teacher's File. |

Writers can
save lives?

See: ● **A5** Reading 'between the lines' (p16)   ● **A16** Argument and persuasion (p49)

Newspapers and magazines often contain articles which they hope will affect the way their readers think and act. This article was prompted by the death of a young woman in tragic circumstances.

WARNING FOR ANYONE TEMPTED BY STEROIDS

The drugs took 10 years to destroy Zoe's superb physique

By the end of her short life Zoe Warwick's internal organs were crumbling, her face was sunken, her teeth had fallen out and she looked 70. And all because she wanted a body beautiful ...

5

Preparation

First impressions

Before you read any further:

1 What is this article going to be about?
2 How does the picture fit in with the two statements written beside it?
3 Giving reasons for your answer, decide whether it is an effective way to begin an article.

Now read the article. As you read, write notes in answers to the questions, so that you can talk and write about it afterwards.

10   Every time we met, Zoe Warwick said: 'I'm dying. I know that. I don't want to die but maybe others can learn from my mistakes. It's too late for me.' And now Zoe is dead. At 35, she had the body of a 70-year old.

15   Steroids were slowly, painfully, burning her away from the inside out. Her liver, kidneys and heart were all packing up.

Illegal steroids – available like Smarties to so many young athletes in gyms and changing rooms across Britain – did that to her.

20   Death came after years of pain and Zoe was so angry about that.

Anger kept her alive for years. She was angry when I first met her during an investigation into the illegal sale of steroids.

25   And she became angrier as the years went on because she saw what they were doing to other youngsters – and how little is being done to clamp down on the horrible trade.

'Why don't the politicians realise that steroids are as
30   dangerous and insidious as heroin and crack?' she raged.

Steroids took 10 years to kill her. But they got her eventually. And I watched during those years as they turned a bubbling young woman into a crippled geriatric.

During that time, Zoe became a one-woman
35   campaign against steroid abuse and the dealers who make a lucrative living from their sale. She talked to newspapers, appeared on television and lobbied Parliament.

Steroids built her up to become even bigger after she
40   won the British Women's Bodybuilding Championship and at one time she was ranked fourth in the world. Then they drained her life.

Hers was an extreme case, she was the first to admit, but not that extreme. The message she kept hammering
45   home was that the designer drugs are still out there, for footballers, rugby players and track athletes, as well as those who need the bulk for power sports such as the shot, javelin, discus and, of course, bodybuilding.

And without tough legislation the trade won't stop.
50   Drugs barons are always ahead of the athletics authorities in ways to avoid detection she emphasised.

Preparation

Zoe's fight against steroids

1   What are the facts about how Zoe died?

2   How does the writer impress upon the reader how strongly Zoe felt about:

  a   what had happened to her?
  b   the illegal trade in steroids?

3   Look at some of the phrases the writer uses:

  a   'Illegal steroids' are available 'like Smarties'. Why do you think he compares these drugs to sweets?
  b   'Steroids took 10 years to kill her. But they got her in the end.' What impact does calling drugs 'they' have?
  c   'they turned a bubbling young woman into a crippled geriatric.' How does this convey the horror of how Zoe changed?

insidious (line 30): unseen but deadly
geriatric (line 33): old
lobbied (line 37): tried to persuade Members of Parliament to act to change the law

On the phone, Zoe sounded like a man. Her voice was the first thing to go on steroids – about two octaves lower. Her jaw jutted out. She grew facial hair.

She developed 'steroid rage' – a 5ft 6in woman, with an inner fury built on drugs, wanting to fight it out with 6ft men, knowing she was strong enough to beat them. 'I wanted to deck anyone who argued with me,' she said.

Her muscles pumped up, which was the object of the exercise. But at that time, in the early Eighties, Zoe did not realise the damage the pills she popped every day were wreaking on her internal organs. That would take more time to show.

Always a good athlete she had a lust for life and a thirst for success. The RAF realised this when she left school with two A-levels and applied for a job. They sponsored her for a degree in sports science and, when she graduated, she joined up as a physical training inspector.

Studying the effects of exercise and diet, Zoe developed a fascination for bodybuilding.

'I wanted to see just how much I could improve my body,' she said. 'I wanted perfection, to be the best. I trained in the gym four hours a day, ran 12 or 15 miles in the evening. I weighed 11 stone and could bench-press 200 kilos easily.'

But when she went to America as the reigning British women's bodybuilding champion, she realised that all her dedication to diet and pumping iron was a waste of time when she compared her physique to 'chemically enhanced' bodies.

Back in London, one day in her gym a man said he could 'course her up'. So, in her ignorance and terrified of injections, Zoe swallowed steroids by the handful.

'That was my first dreadful mistake,' she said. 'Either way steroids will get you in the end but taken orally they get you faster.'

She explained in great detail how, in pill form, steroids go through the system twice – attacking the liver twice. She was on the drugs for 14 months, mostly the male hormone testosterone.

Preparation

The effects of steroid abuse

1 What facts are there in this section about what taking steroids can do to an athlete? Look at:

■ the good things
■ the bad things.

2 How does Zoe appear in the photograph compared to the description in this section?
3 How did steroids change her personality?
4 How do you think the journalist feels towards Zoe?
5 Pick out some sentences or phrases and explain how they reveal his feelings.

Reasons for wanting to take steroids

What are the reasons which made Zoe the sort of person who would be interested in taking steroids?

wreaking (line 62): inflicting/causing
chemically enhanced (lines 80–81): the improvements came from taking chemicals (drugs)

In that short time it wasn't just her liver that was ruined. A year before she died, every internal organ in Zoe's body was packing up. She had liver, kidney and heart problems.

At first doctors thought she had Aids because she looked so bad, but tests proved negative.

Specialists tried all kinds of drugs to replace the steroids her body craved, and repair the damage they had done. All to no avail.

Two years ago all her teeth fell out. Her cheeks were sucked in and shrunken, like the skull of a corpse.

After that she did not want any more photos taken. Her muscular 11 stones faded to six and a half stones.

'I'm dying,' said Zoe the last time I saw her. 'I don't want other young people to make the same mistake.'

'Tell them to stay off steroids.'

Barry Wigmore: *Today*

Death by drugs

1 Explain in your own words what the phrase 'course you up' means.
2 Why do you think Zoe took steroids?
3 What does Zoe mean when she says that swallowing steroids was only her 'first dreadful mistake'?
4 Which words or phrases do you think are the most effective at showing the unpleasant effects of the steroids upon Zoe's body? Give reasons for your choice.
5 Why do you think Barry Wigmore includes the fact that at first the doctors thought she was suffering from AIDS when describing the effects the drugs had on her?
6 Why do you think Barry Wigmore ends his article with Zoe's last words to him?
7 Choosing from all the things Zoe says in the whole article, explain which of her words you think have most effect.

Thinking and writing about the article as a whole

The title of the article is: *Warning for anyone tempted by steroids*. Write an answer to this question:

How successfully does the article warn people against taking steroids?

In order to help you give a detailed and well thought through answer you should consider the following points:

■ How clear is the picture in the article of what steroids can do to athletes?
■ What are the different methods Barry Wigmore has used to warn his reader against taking steroids?
■ Which facts, words, phrases, or images did you find most powerful? Give reasons for your choice.
■ For what reasons does someone take steroids?
■ Does the article do enough to persuade someone thinking of taking steroids that it is not worth it?

Preparation

Selecting and using information

The article you read was aimed at a particular audience and written for a particular purpose.

- What audience was it aimed at?
- How would you describe its purpose?

The same information could be used for different purposes and aimed at different audiences. To write effectively, a writer needs to ask:

- What am I writing about?
- Why am I writing?
- Who am I writing for?

Practice

Writing

Remember these questions when you tackle these two assignments:

1 You are a doctor researching the use of steroids in medicine as well as the effects of steroid abuse. Write a brief factual account of both the beneficial (helpful) and harmful effects of taking steroids, for a magazine which will be read by doctors who treat young people. Include any information you have which might help a doctor spot an athlete misusing steroids.
2 Zoe wanted to make politicians realise that steroids were just as bad as other illegal drugs such as 'heroin and crack'. She believed that more should be done to stop drug dealers selling steroids. Write a letter to your MP expressing this argument and using the facts of her life as your evidence.

A different story

1 Zoe and Barry Wigmore hoped that by knowing about Zoe and the awful effect taking steroids had on her, other young people would be prevented from making the same mistake.

    Imagine a promising young athlete, who has read the article, is approached by the same man who sold the steroids to Zoe. With a partner act out the conversation which could take place.

    - Think carefully about what arguments the pusher would put forward to make a sale.
    - Think carefully about why the athlete might be tempted, but also what reasons there are for resisting.

2 Design a poster which could be displayed in changing rooms to persuade young people not to take steroids.

TF There is an exam practice paper and mark scheme for this unit in the Teacher's File.

Rumours about you

B11

See: ● **A5** Reading 'between the lines' (p16)
● **A20** Character (p62)
● **A21** Action! (p66)

'Sit down, young man,' said the Official.

'Thanks.' The young man sat.

'I've been hearing rumours about you,' the Official said pleasantly. 'Oh, nothing much. Your nervousness. Your not
5 getting on so well. Several months now I've heard about you, and I thought I'd call you in. Thought maybe you'd like your job changed. Like to go overseas, work in some other War Area? Desk job killing you off, like to get right in on the old fight?'

10 'I don't think so,' said the young sergeant.

'What *do* you want?'

The sergeant shrugged and looked at his hands. 'To live in peace. To learn that during the night, somehow, the guns of the world had rusted, the
15 bacteria had turned sterile in their bomb casings, the tanks had sunk like prehistoric monsters into roads suddenly made tar pits. That's what I'd like.'

sterile: harmless, unable to infect with germs

'That's what we'd all like, of course,' said
20 the Official. 'Now stop all that idealistic chatter and tell me where you'd like to be sent. You have your choice – the Western or Northern War Zone.' The Official tapped a pink map on his desk.

25 But the sergeant was talking at his hands, turning them over, looking at the fingers: 'What would you officers do, what would we men do, what would the *world* do if we all woke tomorrow with the guns in flaking ruin?'

30 The Official saw that he would have to deal carefully with the sergeant. He smiled quietly. 'That's an interesting question. I like to talk about such theories, and my answer is that there'd be mass panic. Each nation would think

35 itself the only unarmed nation in the world, and would blame its enemies for the disaster. There'd be waves of suicide, stocks collapsing, a million tragedies.'

'But *after* that,' the sergeant said. 'After they

40 realised it was true, that every nation was disarmed and there was nothing more to fear, if we were all clean to start over fresh and new, what then?'

'They'd re-arm as swiftly as possible.'

45 'What if they could be stopped?'

'Then they'd beat each other with their fists. If it got down to that. Huge armies of men with boxing gloves of steel pikes would gather at the national borders. And if you took the gloves

pikes: spears

50 away they'd use their fingernails and feet. And if you cut their legs off they'd *spit* on each other. And if you cut off their tongues and stopped their mouths with corks they'd fill the atmosphere so full of hate that mosquitoes

55 would drop to the ground and birds would fall dead from telephone wires.'

'Then you don't think it would do any good?' the sergeant said.

'Certainly not. It'd be like ripping the

60 carapace off a turtle. Civilisation would gasp and die from shock.'

carapace: shell

The young man shook his head. 'Or are you lying to yourself and me because you've a nice comfortable job?'

65 'Let's call it ninety per cent cynicism, ten per cent rationalising the situation. Go put your Rust away and forget about it.'

cynicism: not believing in goodness

The sergeant jerked his head up. 'How'd you know I *had* it?' he said.

70 'Had what?'
    'The Rust, of course.'
    'What're you talking about?'
    'I *can* do it, you know. I could start the Rust tonight if I wanted to.'
    The Official laughed. 'You can't be serious.'
75 'I am. I've been meaning to come talk to you. I'm glad you called me in.
    I've worked on this invention for a long time. It's been a dream of mine. It
    has to do with the structure of certain atoms. If you study them you find that
    the arrangement of atoms in steel armour is such-and-such an arrangement.
    I was looking for an imbalance factor. I majored in physics and metallurgy,
80 you know. It came to me, there's a Rust factor in the air all the time. Water
    vapour. I had to find a way to give steel a "nervous breakdown". Then the
    water vapour everywhere in the world would take over. Not on all metal, of
    course. Our civilisation is built on steel, I wouldn't want to destroy most
    buildings. I'd just eliminate guns and shells, tanks, planes, battleships. I can
85 set the machine to work on copper and brass and aluminium, too, if
    necessary. I'd just walk by all of those weapons and just being near them I'd
    make them fall away.'

metallurgy: the study of metals

Preparation

The story so far ...

1 What do you think is the job of the Official?
2 What is the sergeant's job?
3 What does the sergeant want to do?
4 How does he think he can do it?
5 What impression do you have of the Official as a person?

The Official was bending over his desk, staring at the sergeant. 'May I ask you a question?'

'Yes.'

'Have you ever thought you were Christ?'

'I can't say that I have. But I have considered that God was good to me to let me find what I was looking for, if that's what you mean.'

The Official reached into his breast pocket and drew out an expensive ball-point pen capped with a rifle shell. He flourished the pen and started filling in a form. 'I want you to take this to Dr Mathews this afternoon, for a complete check-up. Not that I expect anything really bad, understand. But don't you feel you *should* see a doctor?'

'You think I'm lying about my machine,' said the sergeant. 'I'm not. It's so small it can be hidden in this cigarette package. The effect of it extends for nine hundred miles. I could tour this country in a few days, with the machine set to a certain type of steel. The other nations couldn't take advantage of us because I'd rust their weapons as they approach us. Then I'd fly to Europe. By this time next month the world would be free of war forever. I don't know how I found this invention. It's impossible. Just as impossible as the atom bomb. I've waited a month now, trying to think it over. I worried about what would happen if I did rip off the carapace, as you say. But now I've just decided. My talk with you has helped clarify things. Nobody thought an aeroplane would ever fly, nobody thought an atom would ever explode, and nobody thinks that there can ever be Peace, but there *will* be.'

'Take that paper over to Dr Mathews, will you?' said the Official hastily.

The sergeant got up. 'You're not going to assign me to any new Zone then?'

'Not right away, no. I've changed my mind. We'll let Mathews decide.'

'I've decided then,' said the young man. 'I'm leaving the post within the next few minutes. I've a pass. Thank you very much for giving me your valuable time, sir.'

'Now look here, Sergeant, don't take things so seriously. You don't have to leave. Nobody's going to hurt you.'

'That's right. Because nobody would believe me. Goodbye, sir.' The sergeant opened the office door and stepped out.

The door shut and the Official was alone. He stood for a moment looking at the door. He sighed. He rubbed his hands over his face. The phone rang. He answered it abstractedly.

'Oh, *hello*, Doctor. I was just going to call you.' A pause. 'Yes, I was going to send him over to you. Look, is it all right for that young man to be wandering about? It *is* all right? If you say so, Doctor. Probably needs a rest, a good long one. Poor boy has a delusion of rather an interesting sort. Yes, yes. It's a shame. But that's what a Sixteen-Year War can do to you, I suppose.'

The phone voice buzzed in reply.

The Official listened and nodded. 'I'll make a note on that. Just a second.' He reached for his ball-point pen. 'Hold on a moment. Always mislaying things.' He patted his pocket. 'Had my pen here a moment ago. Wait.' He put down the phone and searched his desk, pulling out drawers. He checked his blouse pocket again. He stopped moving. Then his hands twitched slowly into his pocket and probed down. He poked his thumb and forefinger deep and brought out a pinch of something.

He sprinkled it on his desk blotter: a small filtering powder of yellow-red rust.

He sat staring at it for a moment. Then he picked up the phone. 'Mathews,' he said, 'get off the line, quick.' There was a click of someone hanging up and then he dialled another call. 'Hello, Guard Station, listen, there's a man coming past you any minute now, you know him, name of Sergeant Hollis, stop him, shoot him down, kill him if necessary, don't ask questions, kill the son of a bitch, you heard me, this is the Official talking! Yes, kill him, you hear!'

'But sir,' said a bewildered voice on the other end of the line. 'I can't, I just *can't* ...'

'What do you mean, you can't, God damn it!'

abstractedly: with his mind on other things

delusion: strange and confused idea

filtering: fine

bewildered: puzzled, confused

'Because ...' the voice faded away. You could hear the guard breathing into the phone a mile away.

The Official shook the phone. 'Listen to me, listen, get your gun ready!'

'I can't shoot anyone,' said the guard.

5   The Official sank back in his chair. He sat blinking for half a minute, gasping.

Out there even now – he didn't have to look, no one had to tell him – the hangars were dusting down in soft red rust, and the aeroplanes were blowing away on a brown-rust wind into nothingness, and the tanks were sinking, sinking slowly into the hot asphalt roads, like dinosaurs (isn't that what the man had said?) sinking into primordial tar pits. Trucks were blowing away in ochre puffs of smoke, their drivers dumped by the road, with only the tyres left running on the highways.

asphalt: tarmac
primordial: from the beginning of time
ochre: earth-coloured

'Sir ...' said the guard, who was seeing all this, far away. 'Oh, God ...'

'Listen, listen!' screamed the Official. 'Go after him, get him, with your hands, choke him, with your fists, beat him, use your feet, kick his ribs in, kick him to death, do anything, but get that man. I'll be right out!' He hung up the phone.

By instinct he jerked open the bottom desk drawer to get his service pistol. A pile of brown rust filled the new leather holster. He swore and leaped up.

On the way out of the office he grabbed a chair. It's wood, he thought. Good old-fashioned wood, good old-fashioned maple. He hurled it against the wall twice, and it broke. Then he seized one of the legs, clenched it hard in his fist, his face bursting red, the breath snorting in his nostrils, his mouth wide. He struck the palm of his hand with the leg of the chair, testing it. 'All right, God damn it, come on!' he cried. He rushed out, yelling, and slammed the door.

Ray Bradbury

Preparation

Overview

The story is ...

Look at the following statements which try to sum up the story.

Rank them in order with the best one first.

Say why you have put them in the order you chose.

(If you are doing this as a group, try to reach a unanimous agreement.)

A The story is about war
B The story is about fear
C The story is about dreams

What other statement could you make about the story? Add at least one more 'The story is about ...' sentence of your own.

Titles

One of the five titles below is the title that Ray Bradbury gave to his story.

Which one would you have chosen? Why?

a *The Official View*
b *A Piece of Wood*
c *Sixteen Years*
d *Rust*
e *Peace Panic*

Create another title for the story and say why you chose it.

Understanding the story

Write note-form answers to these questions:

1 What evidence is there that the Official actually prefers war to peace? You might look at:

  ■ how he talks about the possibility of peace on page 141, lines 30 to 67
  ■ how he talks to the guard on pages 144–145, lines 143 to 166
  ■ how he behaves at the end of the story on page 145 from line 167 onwards.

2 How does the Official treat the young sergeant? You might look at:

  ■ how he talks to him in the first 38 lines of the story on pages 140–141
  ■ how he responds to the idea of the rust on pages 141–142, lines 65 to 74
  ■ his telephone conversation with the doctor on page 144, lines 125 to 130
  ■ his instructions to the guard and his own behaviour at the end of the story on page 145, lines 164 to 174.

3 What do you think the writer of this story wants to tell us about war and peace? What evidence can you find for your opinion?

Literature assignment

Write an appreciation of the story. Use the ideas you have already worked out and the notes you have made. You should include the following points:

1 a short account of what happens in the story
2 a description of the characters in it
3 an explanation of the views of the young sergeant about war
4 an explanation of the Official's views about war
5 what you think the story is saying about humanity and war
6 how successful you think the story is and why.

Your own writing

Ray Bradbury's story is one of those which asks one of the great 'What if ..?' questions. Here are some more.

■ What if you only came to school when you wanted to?
■ What if there was no school at all?
■ What if there were no cars?
■ What if there was no television?
■ What if all criminals could be caught by a computer?
■ What if young people grew up together without their parents?
■ What if there were no politicians?

Write your own story in which someone has the power to make one of these things happen, or one of them has happened.

B12 Vanessa, Sandy and Doris

See: **A5** Reading 'between the lines' (p16) ● **A20** Character (p62) ● **A23** Dialogue in literature (p74)

In this unit, you will have the chance to look at the opening of two plays and to work on some scripts of your own.

What if it's positive?

Characters: Vanessa Claythorpe, Sandy Barrett, Mrs Claythorpe

SCENE 1 *A bedroom.*

SANDY and VANESSA enter.

> VANESSA: You sit on the chair, Sand. I'll sit on the bed.
> SANDY: Your mum's out?
> VANESSA: She's at my auntie's. Won't be back for ages. Thanks for coming. I couldn't go through this on my own.

5

The Heinemann English Programme 4 – Foundation

SANDY: You did the test right?

VANESSA: First thing this morning. Like it said. What if it's positive? I'll kill myself, Sand! I will!

SANDY: Don't even talk like that. Where is it?

10 VANESSA: The test, you mean? In that drawer behind my jumpers. Will you look to see what colour it is?

SANDY: (*Rising*) Right. May as well get it over with.

VANESSA: If it's pink I'm all right. Please God, don't let it be ... Please.

SANDY: What's that Steve say about this? After all, it's his fault.

15 VANESSA: I've not told him. I can't blame him. We're usually so careful.
(*SANDY opens drawer.*)

SANDY: Well, it only takes once.

VANESSA: The test, Sand? What colour?

SANDY: It's pink, Van. It's pink!

20 VANESSA: Let's have a look. (*Takes test.*) Thank God. If I'd been pregnant I'd have killed myself, Sand.

SANDY: Forget that. Let's celebrate. Have a liquorice allsort!
(*She gives VANESSA one from a bag, and eats the last herself.*)

VANESSA: Ta. Here, I'd better get rid of this test.

25 SANDY: Put it in this paper bag.

VANESSA: If me mum found it I wouldn't have to kill myself.
          She'd do it for me.

SANDY: You can't go through this every month, Van. You'll
          have to go on the pill.

30 VANESSA: I was going to go to me doctor. But Helen Marshall,
          she went to him. He was a bit sticky.

SANDY: How d'you mean?

VANESSA: He tried to persuade her to talk it over with her
          mother. So she just walked out.

35 SANDY: Well, that was a bit silly.

VANESSA: I'd have done the same. Does your mum know, Sand,
          that you're sleeping with Pete, that you're on't pill?

SANDY: No. She's not as bad as your mum. But I don't know
          how she'd take it.

40 VANESSA: I think it's the fact that my father's dead, that she's on
          her own, that makes mum like she is. She doesn't want
          me to have a life of my own, always prying into what
          I'm doing, what I'm thinking even –

SANDY: I'd not put up with that.

45 VANESSA: I just lie, tell her what she wants to hear. What else
          can I do?

SANDY: Look, Nessa, about the pill. Come to the clinic where
          I go. They're all right there.

VANESSA: I don't know –

50 SANDY: It's better than getting pregnant, than
          you thinking about killing yourself!

	VANESSA:	Yeah. I'll go. Will you come with me?
	SANDY:	I'll even make the appointment for you. Just be careful, though, your mum doesn't find the pills.
55		I always keep mine on me.
	VANESSA:	Let's have a look.
	SANDY:	They're in me bag. (*She hands them over.*) Here.
	VANESSA:	Amazing. Such a tiny pill can stop you getting pregnant.
60		(*MRS CLAYTHORPE enters.*)
	MRS CLAYTHORPE:	I thought I heard voices –
	VANESSA:	(*Horrified*) Mum!

Kara May: *Family frictions*

Looking at the opening

Write notes in answer to these questions, so that you can use them later:

1 What do you learn about the situation between Vanessa and her mother?
2 How would you describe Vanessa's character?
3 In what ways is Sandy different from Vanessa?

Director's cut

Suppose you were in charge of a stage or television performance of this scene. How could you direct it to get the best out of it?
Make notes about:

1 what the characters might wear
2 how they might move – and when
3 how they might say their lines
4 what the set might look like.

Practice

What next?

What might happen next if this scene continued?
What other scenes might you have in this play?

1 Think of as many possibilities as you can.
2 Choose the best ones to create a short storyline for the play you would like to see written.
3 Write up one of the scenes.

Doris

This is the first part of a play called *A cream cracker under the settee.* The play is unusual in that it is a series of monologues – speeches for the one character, Doris.

Doris is in her seventies and the play is set in the living-room and hallway of her semi-detached house. She is sitting slightly awkwardly on a low chair and rubbing her leg. Morning.

It's such a silly thing to have done.

5 *Pause*

I should never have tried to dust. Zulema says to me every time she comes, 'Doris. Do not attempt to dust. The dusting is my department. That's what the council pay me for. You are now a lady of leisure. Your dusting days are over.' Which would be all
10 right provided she did dust. But Zulema doesn't dust. She half-dusts. I know when a place isn't clean.

The Heinemann English Programme 4 – Foundation

Preparation

Questions

1 What 'silly thing' might she have done?
2 Who could Zulema be?
3 What is your first impression of Doris?
4 What might her voice be like?

When she's going she says, 'Doris. I don't want to hear that you've been touching the Ewbank. The Ewbank is out of bounds.' I said, 'I could just run round with it now and again.' She said, 'You can't run anywhere.
15 You're on trial here.' I said, 'What for?' She said, 'For being on your own. For not behaving sensibly. For not acting like a woman of seventy-five who has a pacemaker and dizzy spells and doesn't have the sense she was born with.' I said, 'Yes, Zulema.'

She says, 'What you don't understand, Doris, is that I am the only
20 person that stands between you and Stafford House. I have to report on you. The Welfare say to me every time, "Well, Zulema, how is she coping? Wouldn't she be better off in Stafford House?"'

I said, 'They don't put people in Stafford House just for running round with the Ewbank.' 'No,' she says. 'They bend over backwards to
25 keep you in your own home. But, Doris, you've got to meet them half-way. You're seventy-five. Pull your horns in. You don't have to swill the flags. You don't have to clean the bath. Let the dirt wait. It won't kill you. I'm here every week.'

I was glad when she'd gone, dictating. I sat for a bit looking up at me
30 and Wilfred on the wedding photo. And I thought, 'Well, Zulema, I bet you haven't dusted the top of that.' I used to be able to reach only I can't now. So I got the buffet and climbed up. And she hadn't. Thick with dust. Home help. Home hindrance. You're better off doing it yourself. And I was just wiping it over when, oh hell, the flaming buffet went over.

35 *Pause*

You feel such a fool. I can just hear Zulema. 'Well, Doris, I did tell you.' Only I think I'm all right. My leg's a bit numb but I've managed to get back on the chair. I'm just going to sit and come round a bit. Shakes you up, a fall.

40 *Pause*

Shan't let on I was dusting.

She shoves the duster down the side of the chair.

Dusting is forbidden.

She looks down at the wedding photo on the floor.

45 Cracked the photo. We're cracked, Wilfred.

Pause

The gate's open again. I thought it had blown shut, only now it's blown open. Bang bang bang all morning, it'll be bang bang bang all afternoon.

50 Dogs coming in, all sorts. You see Zulema should have closed that, only she didn't.

Ewbank: type of carpet cleaner

swill the flags: wash the path

buffet: small stool

Pause

The sneck's loose, that's the root cause of it. It's wanted doing for years. I kept saying to Wilfred, 'When are you going to get round to that gate?' But oh no. It was always the same refrain. 'Don't worry, Mother. I've got it on my list.' I never saw no list. He had no list. I was the one with the list. He'd no system at all, Wilfred. 'When I get a minute, Doris.' Well, he's got a minute now, bless him.

Pause

Feels funny this leg. Not there.

Pause

Some leaves coming down now. I could do with trees if they didn't have leaves, going up and down the path. Zulema won't touch them. Says if I want leaves swept I've to contact the Parks Department.

    I wouldn't care if they were my leaves. They're not my leaves. They're next-door's leaves. We don't have any leaves. I know that for a fact. We've only got the one little bush and it's an evergreen, so I'm certain they're not my leaves. Only other folks won't know that. They see the bush and they see the path and they think, 'Them's her leaves.' Well, they're not.

    I ought to put a note on the gate. 'Not my leaves.' Not my leg either, the way it feels. Gone to sleep.

Alan Bennett: *A cream cracker under the settee*

sneck: latch

refrain: chorus, reply

Preparation

Questions

5 What does Doris think of Zulema?

6 What do you think Zulema thinks of Doris?

7 What might 'Stafford House' be?

8 What do we learn about Wilfred?

9 What do you think Doris thinks of her neighbours?

10 What do you think Doris's neighbours might think of her?

Getting the voice

What do you think Doris would sound like?

How would she say her lines?

1 Choose a section of about ten lines.
2 Practise reading it aloud. Work on:

- the way you think she might speak
- the speed at which she might speak
- where she might pause.

3 If possible, work in pairs and share ideas to improve your performances.

Doris's story

How might Doris continue her story?
What might she reveal?
If the next scene were one hour or day or week later, what might have happened?
Prepare your own version of the next section of the play.
Try to keep the character and language consistent with the scene you have studied.

Doris and Zulema

What might happen when Zulema next visits Doris?

Work on the dialogue they might have.
To help you, look back at what Doris thinks and what she tells us of their last conversation. Think about:

- their argument about dusting on page 151
- Zulema's remark about the Ewbank (the carpet sweeper) on page 152
- Zulema's warning about the 'Welfare' and 'Stafford House' on page 152
- Zulema's comment about letting the dirt wait on page 152.

Your own character

Create a monologue for your own choice of person.

1 Decide who it will be. Here are some ideas for characters:

- a school inspector
- a new caretaker
- a check-out operator at a local supermarket
- a dentist
- a young person who has just arrived in the area
- a grandparent who has recently moved in to live with their family.

2 Think about the person you have chosen:

- What are they like?
- How do they speak?

3 Write a few lines to get a 'feel' for the character.
4 Think about the situation your character is going to talk about:

- What has been happening to them?
- What do they think?

5 Write your monologue.

B13 TONY KYTES, THE ARCH-DECEIVER

See: ● **A5** Reading 'between the lines' (p16)
● **A20** Character (p62) ● **A21** Action! (p66)

Thomas Hardy (1840–1928) was the first major writer to focus on the countryside and its people. One book of stories was written as if they were tales that were told on a horse-drawn cart returning from town to a local village. The stories are told to someone who is returning after 35 years and wants to know what has happened. The driver of the cart tells the first tale which is about Tony Kytes.

> After you have finished reading the story you will be asked to write about Tony Kytes and the other characters. At stages during the story there are questions to guide your reading. You will find it helpful to make a note of your answers to these questions. You can do this during your first or second reading of the story.

I shall never forget Tony's face. 'Twas a little, round, firm, tight face, with a seam here and there left by the smallpox, but not enough to hurt his looks in a woman's eye, though he'd had it baddish when he was a boy. So very serious looking and unsmiling 'a was, that young man, that it really seemed
5 as if he couldn't laugh at all without great pain to his conscience. He looked very hard at a small speck in your eye when talking to 'ee. And there was no more sign of a whisker or beard on Tony Kytes's face than on the palm of my hand. He used to sing 'The Tailor's Breeches' with a religious manner, as if it were a hymn:—

10 'O the petticoats went off, and the breeches they went on!'

and all the rest of the scandalous stuff. He was quite the women's favourite, and in return for their likings he loved 'em in shoals.

shoals: large numbers

But in course of time Tony got fixed down to one in particular, Milly Richards, a nice, light, small, tender little thing; and it was soon said that
15 they were engaged to be married.

Preparation

Questions

1 What are your first impressions of:

■ what Tony looks like?
■ what he is like as a person?

Unity

One Saturday he had been to market to do business for his father, and was driving home the waggon in the afternoon. When he reached the foot of the very hill we shall be going over in ten minutes who should he see waiting for him at the top but Unity Sallet, a handsome girl, one of the young women he'd been very tender
20 towards before he'd got engaged to Milly.

As soon as Tony came up to her she said, 'My dear Tony, will you give me a lift home?'

'That I will, darling,' said Tony. 'You don't suppose I could refuse 'ee?'

She smiled a smile, and up she hopped, and on drove Tony.

25 'Tony,' she says, in a sort of tender chide, 'why did ye desert me for that other one? In what is she better than I? I should have made 'ee a finer wife, and a more loving one, too. 'Tisn't girls that are so easily won at first that are the best. Think how long we've known each other – ever since we were children almost – now haven't we, Tony?'

chide: complaint

30 'Yes, that we have,' says Tony, a-struck with the truth o't.

'And you've never seen anything in me to complain of, have ye, Tony? Now tell the truth to me!'

'I never have, upon my life,' says Tony.

'And – can you say I'm not pretty, Tony? Now look at me!'

35 He let his eyes light upon her for a long while. 'I really can't,' says he. 'In fact, I never knowed you was so pretty before!'

light: rest

'Prettier than she?'

What Tony would have said to that nobody knows for before he could speak, what should he see ahead, over the hedge past the turning, but a feather he knew well –
40 the feather in Milly's hat – she to whom he had been thinking of putting the question as to giving out the banns that very week.

banns: legal announcement of a wedding

'Unity,' says he, as mild as he could, 'here's Milly coming. Now I shall catch it mightily if she sees 'ee riding here with me; and if you get down she'll be turning the corner in a moment, and, seeing 'ee in the road, she'll know we've been coming on together. Now, dearest Unity, will ye, to avoid all unpleasantness, which I know ye can't bear any more than I, will ye lie down in the back part of the waggon, and let me cover you over with the tarpaulin till Milly has passed? It will all be done in a minute. Do! – and I'll think over what we've said, and perhaps I shall put a loving question to you after all, instead of to Milly. 'Tisn't true that it is all settled between her and me.'

tarpaulin: large canvas sheet

Well, Unity Sallet agreed, and lay down at the back end of the waggon, and Tony covered her over, so that the waggon seemed to be empty but for the loose tarpaulin; and then he drove on to meet Milly.

Preparation

Questions

2 Where does Unity fit in to the story of Tony's love life?
3 In what ways does she encourage him to flirt with her?
4 How does he respond?
5 What do you think of the way in which he behaves when he sees Milly?

Milly

'My dear Tony!' cries Milly, looking up with a little pout at him as he came near. 'How long you've been coming home! Just as if I didn't live at Upper Longpuddle at all! And I've come to meet you as you asked me to do, and to ride back with you, and talk over our future home – since you asked me, and I promised. But I shouldn't have come else, Mr Tony!'

'Ay, my dear, I did ask 'ee – to be sure I did, now I think of it – but I had quite forgot it. To ride back with me, did you say, dear Milly?'

'Well, of course! What can I do else? Surely you don't want me to walk, now I've come all this way?'

'O no, no! I was thinking you might be going on to town to meet your mother. I saw her there – and she looked as if she might be expecting 'ee.'

'O no; she's just home. She came across the fields, and so got back before you.'

'Ah! I didn't know that,' says Tony. And there was no help for it but to take her up beside him.

They talked on very pleasantly, and looked at the trees, and beasts, and birds, and insects, and at the ploughmen at work in the fields, till presently who should they see looking out of the upper window of a house that stood beside the road they were following, but Hannah Jolliver, another young beauty of the place at that time, and the very first woman that Tony had fallen in love with – before Milly and before Unity, in fact – the one that he had almost arranged to marry instead of Milly. She was a much more dashing girl than Milly Richards, though he'd not thought much of her of late. The house Hannah was looking from was her aunt's.

presently: after a while

dashing: smart and lively

The Heinemann English Programme 4 – Foundation

157

'My dear Milly – my coming wife, as I may call 'ee,' says Tony in his modest way, and not so loud that Unity could overhear, 'I see a young woman a-looking out of the window, who I think may accost me. The fact is, Milly, she had a notion that I was wishing to marry her, and since she's
80 discovered I've promised another, and a prettier than she, I'm rather afeard of her temper if she sees us together. Now, Milly, would you do me a favour – my coming wife, as I may say?'

'Certainly, dearest Tony,' says she.

'Then would ye creep under the empty sacks just here in the front of the
85 waggon, and hide there out of sight till we've passed the house? She hasn't seen us yet. You see, we ought to live in peace and goodwill since 'tis almost Christmas, and 'twill prevent angry passions rising, which we always should do.'

'I don't mind, to oblige you, Tony,' Milly said; and though she didn't care
90 much about doing it, she crept under, and crouched down just behind the seat, Unity being snug at the other end. So they drove on till they got near the road-side cottage.

modest: shy and moral
accost: stop
notion: idea

passions: feelings

snug: comfortable

Preparation

Questions

6 Are these statements true or are they misleading? In each case, explain your answer:

a Milly is angry because Tony is late.
b Tony honestly believes that Milly's mother is waiting for her in town.
c Tony tells Milly the truth about Hannah.

Hannah

Hannah had soon seen him coming, and waited at the window, looking down upon him. She tossed her head a little disdainful and smiled off-hand.

'Well, aren't you going to be civil enough to ask me to ride home with you!' she says, seeing that he was for driving past with a nod and a smile.

'Ah, to be sure! What was I thinking of?' said Tony, in a flutter. 'But you seem as if you was staying at your aunt's?'

'No, I am not,' she said. 'Don't you see I have my bonnet and jacket on? I have only called to see her on my way home. How can you be so stupid, Tony?'

'In that case ah – of course you must come along wi' me,' says Tony, feeling a dim sort of sweat rising up inside his clothes. And he reined in the horse, and waited till she'd come downstairs, and then helped her up beside him, her feet outside. He drove on again, his face as long as a face that was a round one by nature well could be. Hannah looked round sideways into his eyes. 'This is nice, isn't it, Tony?' she says. 'I like riding with you.' Tony looked back into her eyes. 'And I with you,' he said after a while. In short, having considered her, he warmed up, and the more he looked at her the more he liked her, till he couldn't for the life of him think why he had ever said a word about marriage to Milly or Unity while Hannah Jolliver was in question. So they sat a little closer and closer, their feet upon the foot-board and their shoulders touching, and Tony thought over and over again how handsome Hannah was. He spoke tenderer and tenderer, and called her 'dear Hannah' in a whisper at last.

disdainful: scornful
civil: polite

'You've settled it with Milly by this time, I suppose?' said she.

'N – no, not exactly.'

'What? How low you talk, Tony.'

'Yes – I've a kind of hoarseness. I said, not exactly.'

'I suppose you mean to?'

'Well, as to that.' His eyes rested on her face, and hers on his. He wondered how he could have been such a fool as not to follow up Hannah. 'My sweet Hannah!' he bursts out, taking her hand, not being really able to help it, and forgetting Milly and Unity, and all the world besides. 'Settled it? I don't think I have!'

'Hark!' says Hannah.

hark: listen

'What?' says Tony, letting go her hand.

'Surely I heard a sort of little screaming squeak under those sacks? Why, you've been carrying corn, and there's mice in this waggon, I declare!' She began to haul up the tails of her gown.

'O no, 'tis the axle,' said Tony in an assuring way. 'It do go like that sometimes in dry weather.'

assuring: confident

'Perhaps it was … Well, now, to be quite honest, dear Tony, do you like her better than me? Because – because, although I've held off so independent, I'll own at last that I do like 'ee, Tony, to tell the truth; and I wouldn't say no if you asked me – you know what.' Tony was so won over by this pretty offering mood of a girl who had been quite the reverse (Hannah had a backward way with her at times, if you can mind) that he just glanced behind, and then whispered very soft, 'I haven't quite promised her, and I think I can get out of it, and ask you that question you speak of.'

backward: reserved, reluctant

'Throw over Milly? – all to marry me! How delightful!' broke out Hannah, quite loud, clapping her hands.' At this there was a real squeak – an angry, spiteful squeak, and afterward a long moan, as if something had broke its heart, and a movement of the empty sacks.

'Something's there!' said Hannah, starting up.

'It's nothing. Really,' says Tony in a soothing voice, and praying inwardly for a way out of this. 'I wouldn't tell 'ee at first, because I wouldn't frighten 'ee. But, Hannah, I've really a couple of ferrets in a bag under there, for rabbiting, and they quarrel sometimes. I don't wish it knowed, as 'twould be called poaching. Oh, they can't get out, bless 'ee – you are quite safe! And – and – what a fine day it is, isn't it, Hannah, for this time of year? Be you going to market next Saturday? How is your aunt now?' And so on, says Tony, to keep her from talking any more about love in Milly's hearing. But he found his work cut out for him, and wondering again how he should get out of this ticklish business, he looked about for a chance. Nearing home he saw his father in a field not far off, holding up his hand as if he wished to speak to Tony.

ticklish: awkward or difficult

'Would you mind taking the reins a moment, Hannah,' he said, much relieved, 'while I go and find out what father wants?'

She consented, and away he hastened into the field, only too glad to get breathing time.

Preparation

Questions

Decide which is the best answer to each of these two questions and
say why you have chosen it.

7 How does Hannah encourage Tony's behaviour?

   a by asking for a lift

   b by saying she likes riding with him

   c by asking him about Milly

   d by being offhand to begin with and then talking sweetly to him.

8 Why does Tony encourage Hannah to think he will marry her?

   a as a joke to annoy Milly

   b because he hasn't promised himself to Milly

   c because he doesn't know what he wants

   d because he is attracted by her beauty.

Mr Kytes

He found that his father was looking at him with rather a
stern eye.

'Come, come, Tony,' says old Mr. Kytes, as soon as his son
was alongside him, 'this won't do, you know.'

'What?' says Tony.

'Why, if you mean to marry Milly Richards, do it, and there's
an end o't. But don't go driving about the country with
Jolliver's daughter and making a scandal. I won't have such
things done.'

'I only asked her – that is, she asked me, to ride home.'

'She? Why, now, if it had been Milly, 'twould have been quite
proper; but you and Hannah Jolliver going about by
yourselves–'

'Milly's there, too, father.'

'Milly? Where?'

'Under the corn-sacks! Yes, the truth is, father, I've got
rather into a nunny-watch, I'm afeard! Unity Sallet is there, too–
yes, at the other end, under the tarpaulin. All three are in that
waggon, and what to do with 'em I know no more than the
dead! The best plan is, as I'm thinking, to speak out loud and
plain to one of 'em before the rest, and that will settle it; not
but what 'twill cause 'em to kick up a bit of a miff, for certain.
Now which would you marry, father, if you was in my place?'

'Whichever of 'em did *not* ask to ride with thee.'

nunny-watch: tangled mess

miff: argument, row

'That was Milly, I'm bound to say, as she only mounted by my invitation. But Milly.'

185 'Then stick to Milly, she's the best – But look at that!' … His father pointed toward the waggon. 'She can't hold that horse in. You shouldn't have left the reins in her hands. Run on and take the horse's head, or there'll be some accident to them maids!'

maids: girls

Tony's horse, in fact, in spite of Hannah's tugging at the reins, had
190 started on his way at a brisk walking pace, being very anxious to get back to the stable, for he had had a long day out. Without another word Tony rushed away from his father to overtake the horse. Now of all things that could have happened to wean him from Milly there was nothing so powerful as his father's recommending her. No; it could not be Milly, after
195 all. Hannah must be the one, since he could not marry all three as he longed to do. This he thought while running after the waggon. But queer things were happening inside.

queer: strange

It was, of course, Milly who had screamed under the sack-bags, being obliged to let off her bitter rage and shame in that way at what Tony was
200 saying, and never daring to show, for very pride and dread o' being laughed at, that she was in hiding. She became more and more restless, and in twisting herself about, what did she see but another woman's foot and white stocking close to her head. It quite frightened her, not knowing that Unity Sallet was in the waggon likewise. But after the fright was over
205 she determined to get to the bottom of all this, and she crept and crept along the bed of the waggon, under the tarpaulin, like a snake, when lo and behold she came face to face with Unity.

'Well, if this isn't disgraceful!' says Milly in a raging whisper to Unity.

''Tis,' says Unity, 'to see you hiding in a young man's waggon like this,
210 and no great character belonging to either of ye!'

'Mind what you are saying!' replied Milly, getting louder. 'I am engaged to be married to him, and haven't I a right to be here? What right have you, I should like to know? What has he been promising you? A pretty lot of nonsense, I expect! But what Tony says to other women is all mere wind,
215 and no concern to me!'

wind: words

'Don't you be too sure!' says Unity. 'He's going to have Hannah, and not you, nor me either; I could hear that.'

Now at these strange voices sounding from under the cloth Hannah was thunderstruck a'most into a swound; and it was just at this time that the
220 horse moved on. Hannah tugged away wildly, not knowing what she was doing; and as the quarrel rose louder and louder, Hannah got so horrified that she let go the reins altogether. The horse went on at his own pace, and coming to the corner where we turn round to drop down the hill to Lower Longpuddle he turned too quick, the off wheels went up the bank,
225 the waggon rose sideways till it was quite on edge upon the near axles, and out rolled the three maidens into the road in a heap. The horse looked round and stood still.

thunderstruck: stunned
swound: a faint

maidens: girls

Preparation

Questions

9 Do you agree with each of these statements?

a Mr Kytes is a respectable man.
b Mr Kytes wants his son to make up his mind.

If you disagree with either of them replace it with
a statement of your own.
Find evidence to support both your statements.

The proposals

When Tony came up, frightened and breathless, he was relieved
enough to see that neither of his darlings was hurt, beyond a few
scratches from the brambles of the hedge. But he was rather alarmed
when he heard how they were going on at one another.

'Don't ye quarrel, my dears – don't ye!' says he, taking off his hat
out of respect to 'em. And then he would have kissed them all round,
as fair and square as a man could, but they were in too much of a
taking to let him, and screeched and sobbed till they was quite spent.

'Now I'll speak out honest, because I ought to,' says Tony, as soon
as he could get heard. 'And this is the truth,' says he. 'I've asked
Hannah to be mine, and she is willing, and we are going to put up the
banns next –'

Tony had not noticed that Hannah's father was coming up behind,
nor had he noticed that Hannah's face was beginning to bleed from
the scratch of a bramble. Hannah had seen her father, and had run to
him, crying worse than ever.

'My daughter is *not* willing, sir!' says Mr. Jolliver hot and strong. 'Be
you willing, Hannah? I ask ye to have spirit enough to refuse him, if yer
virtue is left to 'ee and you run no risk?'

'She's as sound as a bell for me, that I'll swear!' says Tony, flaring
up. 'And so's the others, come to that, though you may think it an
unusual thing in me!'

taking: state
spent: exhausted

163

'I have spirit, and I do refuse him!' says Hannah, partly because her father was there, and partly, too, in a tantrum because of the discovery, and the scar that might be left on her face. 'Little did I think when I was so soft with him just now that I was talking to such a false deceiver!'

deceiver: cheater

'What, you won't have me, Hannah?' says Tony, his jaw hanging down like a dead man's.

'Never – I would sooner marry no – nobody at all!' she gasped out, though with her heart in her throat, for she would not have refused Tony if he had asked her quietly, and her father had not been there, and her face had not been scratched by the bramble. And having said that, away she walked upon her father's arm, thinking and hoping he would ask her again.

Tony didn't know what to say next. Milly was sobbing her heart out; but as his father had strongly recommended her he couldn't feel inclined that way. So he turned to Unity.

'Well, will you, Unity dear, be mine?' he says.

'Take her leavings? Not I!' says Unity. 'I'd scorn it!'

leavings: leftovers

And away walks Unity Sallet likewise, though she looked back when she'd gone some way, to see if he was following her. So there at last were left Milly and Tony by themselves, she crying in watery streams, and Tony looking like a tree struck by lightning.

'Well, Milly,' he says at last, going up to her, 'it do seem as if fate had ordained that it should be you and I, or nobody. And what must be must be, I suppose. Hey, Milly?'

ordained: ordered

'If you like, Tony. You didn't really mean what you said to them?'

'Not a word of it!' declares Tony, bringing down his fist upon his palm.

And then he kissed her, and put the waggon to rights, and they mounted together; and their banns were put up the very next Sunday. I was not able to go to their wedding, but it was a rare party they had, by all account. Everybody in Longpuddle was there almost.

rare: brilliant

Thomas Hardy: *Tony Kytes, the arch-deceiver*

Preparation

Questions

10 Complete each of these statements. If you don't think they can be completed correctly, write a true sentence about that character.

Hannah is not bothered by Tony's cheating, she refuses him out of embarrassment and …

Unity would have forgiven Tony for cheating if …

Milly chooses to marry Tony because …

Who's cheating whom?

Preparation

The alternatives

The story is called *Tony Kytes, the arch-deceiver* so the title might suggest that all the faults are with Tony. But are they?
There are at least three ways you might look at what happens here.

A Tony cannot be trusted and what happens is essentially his fault.
B Tony is weak and the women manipulate him, so, on the whole, they deserve what happens to them.
C Tony, Unity, Milly and Hannah are all equally to blame for what happens.

Which of them do you think is most accurate and why? If you are not satisfied with any of them, write a sentence of your own explaining where you think the responsibility lies and giving your reasons.

Practice/Coursework

Writing

Now you are going to write about your opinion, using the title, 'Tony Kytes: who cheated whom?' Make sure that you include these points in your writing:

1 Introduction
A **very short** explanation of what happens in the story and how it ends.
2 The girls
One paragraph about each of the girls, examining how far each of them was responsible for the difficulties Tony found himself in.
3 Tony
Two or three paragraphs looking at Tony's responsibility.
4 Conclusion
Summing up your own opinion – as you explained it in **The alternatives**.

Mr Kytes

Imagine that Tony's father is talking to a close friend about Tony and his escapade with Unity, Milly and Hannah. He tells the story paying particular attention to his views of the characters of Tony and the three girls. What does he say?

Scenes from a life

If someone in the family gets old photographs out, you know you are going to laugh at some and cringe at others. This unit looks at writing about all kinds of memories, pleasant and unpleasant. As you work through it, you will get the chance to write a series of short pieces about what you remember. All these will be in the form of a first draft. At the end of the unit, there is the chance to develop them into a finished whole.

See: ● **A13** Narration (p38)
● **A14** Description (p42)
● **A15** Explanation (p46)

Preparation

Life so far

What do you remember best about your life so far?

1 Have you moved house? What was your previous house or flat or room like?
2 Who do you remember looking after you when you were young?
3 Who do you remember playing with when you were little?
4 Do you remember any trips or holidays? What were they like?
5 What events do you remember from primary school ... teachers you liked, concerts, trips, visitors to your class?

Make a list of your memories and then share some of them.

I remember ...

Preparation

Shared memories

Work in a group of three or four.

Some memories are personal and some we share with other people. For example, the years of our lives may be marked by memories of:

- television programmes
- pop music
- films
- fashions in clothes and shoes
- toys that were popular.

Think about these things and look at the pictures on this page. What do the members of your group remember about the past few years?

Writing

Now use your list of shared memories as the starting point for a piece of writing. You might decide to write about one particular memory, or you might like to make a list poem: each line starts 'I remember...' and contains a new memory.

What to do

Everyone in the group needs paper and something to write with.

1 Everybody in the group just says whatever they remember and everyone writes it down.
2 No one disagrees, laughs or comments on what other people say.
3 No one starts having a conversation about something else.
4 After about four minutes, ask one person to read through the list. If possible, add some more memories.

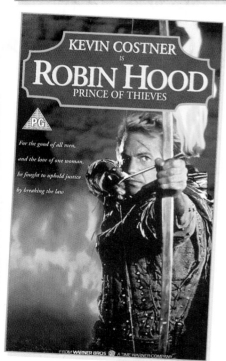

Personal memories

Old photographs, postcards from forgotten holidays, broken toys ...
different things bring back memories for different people. Collect together
one or two things that bring back memories – happy or otherwise – and
bring them to school.

Pair work

Show each other what you have brought and describe the memories they
bring back. Talking about them may bring back details that you had
forgotten. It may even lead you into other memories. Make a note of
anything you remember.

Writing

Use your memories to help you write
a poem. Use the first line to say what
started the memory. Here are four
examples:

- The pencil I bought at Stonehenge
- A torn postcard of Pevensey
- The photo of the team with Jonesey
  looking the wrong way
- The brochure for Heaven Park
  Chalets.

On each line add a little bit more of the memory. Like this:

> The brochure for Heaven Park Chalets –
> It all looked so beautiful in the pictures!
> But when we got there ...
> The mould on the wall in the tiny kitchen,
> The black shrivelled thing we found in the cooker
> That dad said was a mouse
> Which meant we had chips from the shop all week.
> The smell of bacon cooking in the chalet next door
> With the boy who picked his nose
> And then offered you squares of chocolate.

Parties and other disasters

The things that people remember most vividly tend to be the disasters. There's always more to say about things that go wrong than about things that work perfectly. Part of the fun of making friends is in sharing stories about accidents, disasters and emergencies! Joan is now well into her forties but she still recalls her fairly quiet teenage years. Well, quiet except for the one party that she organised.

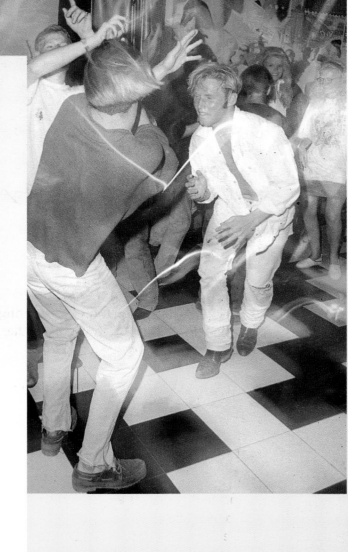

My parents never let us have parties like that, but we did have one once when my mother was away. My mum had gone away to the caravan – that's what they did for their week's holiday – and I kept
5   saying that I didn't want to go. I was 15 and I didn't want to go off to a caravan, so she said she was going off on her own. I think my brother also stayed behind so she just took my younger sister. My elder sister must have been in London by then.
10 Anyway, as soon as she was gone, I organised a party, the only party we ever had at our house at that time. I had to bribe my brother not to tell. We got all the booze in and everything and moved all the furniture out of the way. Then at about
15 1 o'clock in the morning the police turned up looking for somebody. We saw them coming up the path, so what the fellas did was they shoved all the beer bottles under the settee. We thought that you weren't allowed to drink at our age, even indoors,
20 so we didn't want the police to see the beer. The fellas were hiding bottles everywhere and beer got spilled all over the place. Afterwards we couldn't get rid of the smell, and all the police had come for was to get one of the girls. She'd told her mother she
25 was going to a youth club and it was a bit late, so her mother had got them to look for her. That party went on until about 3 a.m.

Joan, talking about her life in Growing up in the 60s by **Cecile Landau**

169

The crazy moments

Think about the things that have happened to you, your friends and your family. Some may seem funny now you look back on them. Others may still make you sad or even angry. Here's a list to help jog your memory:

- a party that went wrong
- a fight
- when the car broke down
- skipping school
- incident with the police
- breaking your arm or leg
- getting in under-age
- in front of the deputy head
- incident at the youth club
- stealing
- trouble with neighbours
- a disaster with a job.

Make a list of what you remember. Put a tick by the memories that you feel are most powerful.

One memory in detail

You have already spent some time recalling your memories. Now is the moment to focus on one event and write about it in a little more detail.

1 Look closely at the memories you have ticked. Choose one to write about.
2 Focus all your attention on that memory.
3 Write down quickly all the details that you can remember. Don't worry about writing complete sentences.
4 Put the parts of your story into the best order you can.
5 Now write your memory.

Did we really say that?

Many biographies are interesting because of the conversations that people remember. Those memories are probably not exactly the words that were said at the time. People's memories are just not that good! But conversation helps to give the atmosphere of what was happening. Valery Avery wrote about growing up in the 1940s. Here she is recalling her friend Janey and one of her ideas.

It was drawing towards Christmas and I had saved five shillings in threepenny bits to buy Mum a brooch, one that sparkled and glittered, a real diamond one. Then one afternoon Janey suggested: 'Let's go to the Astoria, Val, there's a smashing picture on, Mum and Dad saw it last night, they said it was shocking and they don't know how it got past the censor.'

'I can't, Janey, Mum wouldn't let me.'

'You don't have to ask your Mum, do you?'

'She'll find out though. Anyway, where am I gonna get the money from?'

'That's the point. How much you got?'

'Five shillings. But it's not for spending, it's to buy Mum's brooch.'

'You can still buy her one with the money left over. You can get some smashing ones in Woolworth's.'

'But I want to get a proper diamond one in the jeweller's.'

'What's the difference? She won't know where you got it from. It's the thought that counts. Go on, Val, get that five bob out of your tin.'

'No, Janey, not this time. I'll come another time.'

'But there won't be another time. It's only on this week. This is our only chance.'

'No, Janey, I'm not spending that money.'

'All right then. What if we borrow it, just for today. I'm going down my aunt's tomorrow. She always gives me ten bob. I tell you what, Val? If you give up that five bob now, I'll give you ten bob tomorrow.'

'No, you wouldn't, Janey.'

'On me honour I would.'

'Ten bob. I could buy a super one for that, couldn't I?'

'Course you could. Come on, we'll never make it. It starts at half two.'

'But it's all in threepenny bits.'

'Don't matter, it's money all the same, ain't it?'

35 One by one, the threepenny bits came pouring out in a heap and Janey began counting.

'Five shillings – and sixpence. You can't count, Val. See, we're wealthy. Right. Now I'm gonna make meself up because it's an "A" and we
40 mightn't get anyone to take us in.'

'Oh, Janey, do you think we ought? I mean, supposing someone finds out?'

'They won't. I always plan things well, don't I? We went to the park, see, and if
45 we're late back we can say we missed the bus and had to walk. Simple, ain't it? This lipstick on all right?'

Valery Avery: *London morning*

Preparation

Conversations

What do you think you and your friends sound like?
What do you think you and your family sound like?
Think about some situations in which conversations take place.
Try writing up one situation with your friends and one situation with your family.

Here are some possible subjects and scenes:

Friends
- where to go at the weekend
- each other's parents
- sport/rock music/television
- things that have happened
- people you like or dislike
- at a party
- sitting at the back in a lesson
- in the school lunch break.

Family
- which television programme to watch
- the time you have to be in at night
- friends that your parents dislike
- the amount of money you get
- the state of your bedroom
- getting up in the morning
- helping with work in the house
- comparing the past with today.

Preparation

Milestones

So far, you have been looking at moments from your life. How do they fit into your life as a whole? One way of looking at your life is to make a chart of milestones and memories. Use the example below to help you create your own chart.

Year	Where I lived	Milestones	Key memories
1993	23 Baldock Road, Hitchin	We moved from Neasden to Hitchin. I went to Fernhill School.	I hated it at first – everyone was so snooty! Met Carole and we became best friends – she came on holiday with us to the Isle of Wight. Broke my front tooth at the swimming pool.

Possible milestones

starting school
learning to ride a bike
learning to swim
first sleepover
first part-time job
first date

first real friend
first major holiday
changing school
being allowed into town on your own
first trip or holiday without parents
any success at sport

Practice

Writing

Take one event or moment from your chart and try describing it as if it was happening now.
Here is the opening of one 'milestone' to give you an idea.

I never imagined I would ever leave my old school but here I am. I should have eaten some breakfast but I didn't fancy it. Mum shouted at me but I just said nothing. Now I'm starving. There are thousands of us in this hall. Well, it feels like thousands. I bet my name will be missing from the list …

The Heinemann English Programme 4 – Foundation

Bringing it all together

If you have worked through this unit, you will have done
a number of first drafts of different pieces of writing:

- a group poem (page 167)
- lines about a memory (page 168)
- the story of a disaster (page 170)
- conversations (page 172)
- a milestone (page 173).

Plus notes or lists of other memories.

There are two ways to use your notes and your first drafts.

Either:
Make a personal album of memories – a bit like
a photograph album but with words.

1 Read through the writing you have already
   done and re-draft the pieces you want to use.
2 Choose other ideas from your notes and lists
   that you think would fill in any gaps in your
   album. Write them up.
3 Decide on the order for your different pieces.
4 Put it together with some linking words
   between each piece. Parts of your chart
   should help you.
5 If you have them, you could also use old
   photographs to illustrate your work and to
   help make those links.

Or:
Use what you have written so far as the starting
point for a single longer piece of writing.

1 Re-read what you have already written and
   decide which parts you want to use.
2 Choose other ideas from your notes and lists
   that you will use in your writing.
3 Plan the order in which you are going to
   write your memories. It helps to think of
   your writing as a series of chapters in a book
   about yourself.
4 Start writing.

HOT OFF THE PRESS

THIS WAS THE BOXER

THIS WAS THE PLACE

'It all happened so fast. You didn't have enough time to think!'

THESE WERE THE TWO PUPILS WHO BECAME JOURNALISTS IN LESS THAN TWO HOURS

Angela Coughlin and Richard Collins arrived in school as usual one Monday morning expecting to work their normal timetable. Instead, they found the head of English waiting for them. Two people were needed to interview the featherweight champion of the world, Steve Robinson, and to write feature articles on him. Angela and Richard had been 'volunteered'!

'The most difficult thing was coming up with the right sort of questions.'

Local heroes

In this unit you are going to prepare and write an article based on an interview.

Who?

Richard and Angela had a ready-made interview; a world champion boxer had been a pupil at their school and just turned up. But even if you don't happen to know someone famous, it is surprising what fascinating stories you can find through interviewing apparently ordinary people. Here are some suggestions:

School	*Friends and family*	*The local community*
■ a retiring teacher looking back ■ a new teacher looking forward ■ a parent with an unusual job ■ an ex-pupil remembering what the school was like in the past ■ a visitor to the school.	■ someone with an interesting job ■ someone who has just come back from a foreign holiday ■ an older person who can remember what life was like fifty years ago ■ someone who is new to the area.	■ someone who runs an activity in the area – sports clubs, crèches, scouts ■ someone involved in the local religious work – church, mosque, temple, synagogue.

Brainstorming

1 How many people can you think of who might be interviewed?
Make a list of as many as you can.
Use the suggestions from the sections **School**, **Friends and family** and **The local community** to help you find names.
If you are not sure of someone's name, just explain who they are.

2 Decide on the five people from your list who you think would be best in an interview, putting them in order.

Where will your article appear?

You need to think where your article will appear and who will read it.
Choose from this list, or think of your own idea:

■ a local newspaper
■ a school newsletter or magazine
■ a booklet with the title, 'Our community', to be produced locally and distributed in libraries, health centres, and similar places.

Getting the interview

Just because you want to interview someone, doesn't mean that they want to be interviewed. The good news is that many people are quite flattered to be asked. Once they have overcome any nervousness, they enjoy the experience of talking about their lives and experiences. The important thing is to approach them in the right way.

You need to know what you are doing before you contact the person you want to interview. Here is an example of the kind of planning that is required.

Details of person	Mrs Staniforth, 34 Bloxwich Road
What it's about	Her work with handicapped youngsters at day centre – how it started, what she does, why she does it
Reason for doing it	English homework plus interest in doing this sort of work when I leave school
When	any evening next week except Wednesday
Where	at day centre when youngsters have finished? at her house or my nan's house, 32 Bloxwich Road
Time needed	45 minutes maximum

Prepare a grid like the one above for the person you would plan to interview.

Making the approach

If it is someone you know quite well, call on them and just ask. Remember to tell them what the interview is for and what your questions will be about. Have your grid with you when you contact them!

Make sure
- You have told your teacher what you are planning.
- You tell your parents who you are going to interview, why and when.
- You do not go alone to the home of someone you do not know well.

Good interviewing

> **Q:** **How did you feel about school?**
> **A:** I enjoyed school. I thought it was all right.
> **Q:** **Were there any lessons you were particularly good at?**
> 5 **A:** Sport. I loved sport and I never forgot my PE kit. I thought I was a good sportsman, even as a kid.
> **Q:** **Do you have any regrets?**
> **A:** Yes. I regret taking a break from boxing. If I hadn't taken a break and kept on boxing then maybe I
> 10 could have won the World Boxing Organisation Featherweight title at an earlier age.

Part of Angela's interview for Wales on Sunday

Research

Don't miss the chance to ask the right question. The best interviews happen when you know a fair amount about the subject or the person. Collect as much background information as you can.
There are three possible sources for this:

1 your own knowledge – sit and think about the subject carefully
2 asking other people – use friends and family to supply information
3 books and magazines – especially for background information.

Technicalities

When you have prepared for an interview, you want to be sure that you come away from it with good information. The best way of doing this is to use a tape recorder **and** write notes as well.

If you only use a tape recorder, it will go wrong. Ask a journalist! If you only write notes, you may miss something important. You cannot write as fast as people speak.

1 Practise using the tape recorder until you do it automatically.
2 Use new batteries or check you have the plug lead and an extension cable.
3 Make your notes readable.
4 Write out in full any statements you want to quote.
5 Write out carefully any names that may be difficult to spell.

Questions

You need to have a list of questions written down in advance because:

- it makes you sort out your ideas
- you can look at it if your mind goes blank in the interview
- you can check that you have not missed out anything important before you finish.

Good interviewers ask lots of questions that they think of during the interview but their list of questions is an essential back-up.

Question time
1 At the top of page 178, are some of the questions that Angela asked Steve when he was world champion. What else would you have wanted to ask him?
2 Plan the questions you want to ask the person you are interviewing. Use the steps shown in **Preparing your questions**.

Preparing your questions
1 Write down the main areas you want to cover.
2 Write all the possible questions on each area.
3 Put your questions into a sensible order.
4 Make a neat and very clear copy – you have to be able to read them!

Have a practice run

Do a short interview in pairs about moving from your previous school to where you are now. Prepare about six questions but do not rely on them. See if you can get a real conversation going.

When you have done that swap roles, so that the interviewer becomes the person being interviewed.

Doing the interview

1 Turn up on time or a few minutes early.
2 Make the person you are interviewing feel at ease – chat with them generally before the interview. Older people, especially, can feel quite threatened when asked to speak into a microphone.
3 Don't stick rigidly to your list of questions. Follow up what they say. Make it a real conversation.
4 Say thank you at the end.

Now do your interview.

Writing it up

Once you have completed your interview, you need to make the most of your material.

Preparation

1 If you have a tape, listen to it once to get an idea of what it contains. Listen to it again and make notes on the main topics covered. Write down the counter numbers against the topics if you can.
   or
   If you are working from written notes, make a list of the main topics.
2 Decide which topics you want to include in your article.
   For each topic make more detailed notes on what was said in the interview.
3 Decide on the order in which you want to present this material in your article.

Writing a first draft

When you have done this preparation, you are almost ready to write a first draft of your article, but first read the article that Richard produced on Steve Robinson, on page 181.

Now prepare and write the first draft of your own article. Do not forget the audience you are writing for and the place where the article will appear.

STICK AT IT: Champ's message

'We can build a better world'

Steve Robinson

As Wales' world champion boxer Steve Robinson went back to his old, **Glyn Derw High School**, in Ely, Cardiff, to promote BT Environment Week '95, pupil **RICHARD COLLINS** seized the opportunity to interview him about his school days and career

ON a wet Monday morning, Glyn Derw High School, in Ely, Cardiff, welcomed a world champion and released 250 pink heart shaped balloons into the sky as BT announced its environment week.

Steve Robinson, 26, is the featherweight champion of the world, a media megastar and, more importantly, an ex-Glyn Derw pupil.

Now living in Marshfield, Gwent, Steve was brought up in Bromley Drive, Ely, and first got involved in boxing at the age of nine.

"My older brother, Paul, was into boxing at the time and we used to have sparring sessions" he said.

"At that time he always used to win."

Boxing has come in for a lot of criticism recently, but Steve defends it as a sport, claiming it keeps boys off the streets and gives them a sense of self-worth when they are perhaps failing in other areas.

He believes that everyone needs to get that kind of discipline and if, through training hard and showing dedication in the gym, you can gain this, then it is truly a worthy achievement.

At 24, Steve first made the headlines when, against expectations, he became Welsh Boxing champion. From then he has gone on to even greater things and is now World Champion, a title he intends to keep.

Yet such fame has not gone to his head. The first thing you notice about Steve Robinson is a shy, warm smile and a complete lack of arrogance.

He is a family man who cherishes the time spent with his two young sons and cares about people and the world around him. A regular visitor to Glyn Derw, he sets a great example to pupils and is well chosen to promote interest in the environment.

"The world around us is important and we can all do something to preserve and improve our environment," said Steve.

"Young children can help by picking up litter; teenagers can do gardening for elderly neighbours. Little things like that are important and if we all stick at it we can be successful."

Steve has shown how "sticking at it" leads to success. Glyn Derw pupils will respond to BT's call to do their best for the environment. We hope the message spreads.

● Steve Robinson Question and Answer: Page 3
● BT Environment Week competition: Page 3

Wales on Sunday

Editing

In a newspaper or magazine, editing has two main purposes:

- to make an article clearer and easier to understand
- to shorten an article so that it will fit the space available.

There are five main ways in which an article can be edited:

1 by changing the order of sections, so that the whole article follows on in a way that is easier to understand, or more interesting
2 by cutting out whole sections. This can only be done if the section you are cutting out stands on its own and does not have other parts of the article depending on it. In Richard's article on page 181, this paragraph can be cut if necessary:

> Yet such fame has not gone to his head. The first thing you notice about Steve Robinson is a shy, warm smile and a complete lack of arrogance.

3 by cutting words or phrases. This is often done but it takes a lot of time and care to do it well. Look at these examples from Richard's article

> At 24, Steve first made the headlines when, ~~against expectations,~~ he became Welsh Boxing champion. From then he has gone on to even greater things and is now World Champion, ~~a title he intends to keep.~~

> At 24, Steve ~~first made the headlines~~ when, ~~against expectations, he~~ became Welsh Boxing champion. ~~From then he has gone on to even greater things~~ and is now World Champion, ~~a title he intends to keep.~~

4 by adding words to make the meaning clearer
5 by rewriting. Sometimes this is the only way to shorten, or to make something clearer.

Your article

Look again at the first draft of your article.
You do not need to edit this to make it fit into a space in a newspaper.
You do need to cut and change it so that it is as interesting as possible.

> No wasted words, no boring bits.

When you are satisfied with your editing, ask a friend to check it and comment on it. Then make a fair copy.

B16 IN THE HEAT OF THE SUN

See:
- **A8** Purpose (p26)
- **A9, 10** Audience (p28, p31)
- **A15** Explanation (p46)
- **A16** Argument and persuasion (p49)

Voluntary Service Overseas is a development agency sending men and women to share their skills with people in over 55 developing countries. Since 1958, more than 20,000 volunteers have worked overseas with VSO.

This unit is about three people working in Kenya with VSO. It is in three parts:

- **pages 184–187**
  information about the work being done by Rachel Yeats and Gavin Anderson.
  On page 187 there are some questions to answer.

- **pages 188–191**
  Patsy Sterling describes what it is like to be a black female volunteer in Kenya.
  On page 191 there are some questions to answer.

- **page 192**
  a writing activity.

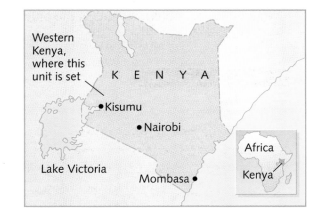

Western Kenya, where this unit is set

KENYA

Kisumu

Nairobi

Lake Victoria

Mombasa

Africa

Kenya

The Heinemann English Programme 4 – Foundation

Gavin and Rachel

Gavin Anderson is an industrial designer from Scotland. His skills are in design and metalworking. Rachel Yeats is also Scottish and is a qualified textile designer, with skills in the designing and making of craft objects. Both of them could have had well-paid jobs with companies in Britain, but they wanted to travel and share their skills with less fortunate people.

Gavin and Rachel applied to VSO together and were given a placement in Kisumu, Western Kenya. They were asked to act as advisers to K.I.C.K. – the Kisumu Innovation Centre, Kenya.

K.I.C.K. is a small organisation which helps poor craftsmen and craftswomen who work for themselves in the Jua Kali.

The Jua Kali

Kenya has a very rapidly growing population. There is a shortage of land for farming, so many young men and women drift into the towns. Unfortunately there are not enough jobs to employ these people – even those who have skills.

Some of the skilled people have joined together and use their skills to manufacture simple objects. They use scrap materials and simple tools – including many they make themselves. They don't have proper workshops and either work in simple sheds, or out in the open in the heat of the sun.

This is how they came to be called the *Jua Kali*. In Kiswahili this means 'the fierce sun'.

Tin briefcases

People in the Jua Kali were making a living, but they only made a small range of different things and there were too many of them making the same thing. Prices were low and as more workers joined in, they had to work harder and harder to earn the same amount of money.

K.I.C.K. gives them advice about:

- other things they could make using the same materials and skills
- how to improve the quality of their products
- how to sell their products.

Gavin advises on many different metal products from carts to office equipment and briefcases.

Wire bicycles and metal birds

Rachel works with artists and craftsmen making ornaments, toys and other craft objects.

Peter Otieno used to be a welder, but the work affected his health and he had to stop. He started making model bicycles and other toys. Rachel has:

- advised him on how to make them better
- suggested different models he can make
- helped him sell them.

Now his models are sold in Nairobi and overseas and Peter earns a lot more money.

Beckans Odongo is a painter. He decorates pots, ornamental boxes and mirrors. Rachel advises him on marketing and design.

The Heinemann English Programme 4 – Foundation

Preparation

Questions

Write two or three sentences in answer to these questions:

1 What skills did Gavin and Rachel bring to their work in Kenya?
2 What is the Jua Kali?
3 How have K.I.C.K., Gavin and Rachel been able to help workers in the Jua Kali?

Patsy Sterling

Most development volunteers in Kenya are white and the majority are men. Patsy Sterling is black and a woman. She worked as an Environmental Health Officer in London for several years before deciding to apply to VSO.

VSO offered Patsy a placement in Western Kenya, as a health educator. At Indangalasia she has:

■ made a survey of the health needs of the community
■ advised people (especially mothers) on primary health care – how people can stay healthy through good hygiene and healthy food
■ started an organic farming project so that people can grow more and better food
■ started a project to help people protect their water supplies so that they always have clean water.

Read the following interview with Patsy and then look at the questions on page 191.

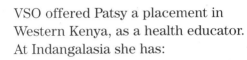

Black mzungu

What is it like being a black volunteer?

'There are positives and negatives to being a black person here. For example, the Kenyans all think that I'm a Kenyan, which is nice, but the downside is that they expect me to speak the various Kenyan languages.'

Because of her life and background she lives a very different life from the local women.

5 'Even if I didn't open my mouth they'll know I'm a stranger, but they'll still react to me differently than they do to the whites who they call *mzungus* here.

'They seem to expect more from me as a fellow black person. When they see me, they see an African and their expectations are completely different. If I'm in the market and they've told me it's ten shillings for a cabbage and I know it's only five shillings, I want to give them five shillings. They get very upset because they feel somehow that I'm doing them out of this five shillings. But if I'd been a mzungu and I'd bartered them down to five shillings they would have great respect for me. They see me as a black mzungu.'

bartered: haggled over the price

An honorary male

What is it like being a woman in a society dominated by men?

'The fact that I ride around on a motorcycle and am a woman is blowing quite a few people's minds. I don't act or behave the same way as the other women do here. I live on my own in a house. I don't have any children, I don't have a husband: therefore I'm a 'Miss' and I'm 'missing' – that's the local term.'

20

Men discussing local affairs at the village *baraza* (meeting)

'They've accepted me, but in differing ways. The older men accept me as an honorary male because I do not act the same way as the women. The things that I do – riding a motorcycle, managing a project, going out and being outspoken with the chief or other people in power – are male things. So their way of accepting me is to treat me as an honorary male.'

25

honorary: someone who is awarded a title (in this example of 'male') as an honour

The challenge

Patsy lives all on her own in a small, simple house with no hot water. For a whole year's work she is paid as much as she used to earn in one month in London. Why does she do it?

'I believe in what VSO is doing. Their idea is to help people share skills, ideas, and knowledge with people from a developing country. Volunteers learn new ideas and skills that we can also use when we get back home. I felt that although I have a lot to give, there was also a lot that I wanted to learn. I wanted to find out what it's like being in a situation where I'm totally on my own. I have to rely on myself for company and entertainment. It was a challenge and I think I've risen to the challenge quite well. I've learned a lot about myself.'

Preparation

Questions

Write two or three sentences to answer these:

1 What work has Patsy Sterling done in Kenya?
2 What does she mean when she describes herself as a 'black mzungu'?
3 How does her behaviour 'blow people's minds' and how do the men deal with it?
4 What does she say she has gained from doing VSO?

Advertising VSO

VSO depends on charitable donations for part of its funds. You have been given the task of preparing a new appeal for funds. It is to be in the form of an A5 leaflet. It will be sent out to possible donors. It will also be distributed in certain newspapers and magazines.

You have been given the material about Rachel, Gavin, and Patsy to form the basis of your appeal.

Thinking

As you think about each of these questions, make a list of the main points you think of:

1 What are the main aims of VSO?
2 Why do they need the money and how will they spend it?
3 How do you think the Kenyans at K.I.C.K. and in the Jua Kali feel about the contribution that Rachel and Gavin are making?
4 How do the people at Indangalasia feel about what Patsy is doing?
5 What advantage is there for people in Britain – why should they support an organisation like VSO?

Planning

1 Look at the notes you have made – and any other writing you have done. Decide what you want to **say** in your appeal.
2 Look back through the photographs in this unit. Decide what illustrations you want to use.
3 Take a piece of A4 paper and fold it in two to make it A5:

Use this to plan your leaflet. Mark on it where you are going to put different parts of your text and where the photographs will go.

Drafting

Now write a rough draft of your appeal. If possible, discuss it with someone else. Read it through carefully to make sure that it says clearly what you want to say. Change it as necessary.

Final version

Now write the text of your final version.